# LORD,
# SOMETIMES
# I NEED
# HELP!

# LORD, SOMETIMES I NEED HELP!

*William L. Coleman*

HAWTHORN BOOKS, INC.
*W. Clement Stone, Publisher*
NEW YORK

*Dedicated to*
*Dr. John H. Mulholland*

# Contents

# Acknowledgments

New Testament quotations in chapters 7, 15, 16, 17, 18, 19, 21, 22, and 23 are from the New International Version, copyright © 1973 by the New York Bible Society, published by Zondervan Publishing House and used by permission. Bible quotations in other chapters are from the King James Version unless indicated otherwise.

Quotations from *The Living Bible*, copyright © 1971 by Tyndale House, are used by permission of the publisher.

Acknowledgment is also made to the following publications in which the original versions of some of the chapters appeared: *Eternity* for the chapters, "Sometimes I Am a Failure" and "Will Everything Really Work Out?"; *Sunday Digest*, David C. Cook, publishers, for "Sometimes I Feel Guilty" and "Sometimes I Get Angry"; *Good News Broadcaster* for "Sometimes I Feel Useless" and "Sometimes I Am Afraid"; *High*, Harvest Publications, publisher, for "Sometimes I Am Confused"; and *Living Today*, Scripture Press, publishers, for "Sometimes I Hold Grudges."

# LORD,
# SOMETIMES
# I NEED
# HELP!

# Welcome!

It is difficult to say just what provokes a person to pick up a book like this. Maybe the cover is the right color, the title is catchy, or else it is a last-minute gift for Aunt Selma in Beaver Crossing.

Whatever the reason for perusing it, hopefully it will soon become a friend who can talk to you because it knows how you feel. Maybe it can unlock a few doors, sweep away some cobwebs or clean off a window to let the sun shine into a soul that has become damp and stuffy.

Certain people will find very little growth from this small volume. Those who are cocksure and reeking with confidence, like a boxer about to conquer all challengers, will consider it pedestrian. It will prove of no lasting assistance to the serious neurotic or borderline psychotic whose wounds are deep and the healing of them complex.

Rather, these chapters are addressed to the broad world of the average person: the neighborhood where we all struggle in life. It is for the person who gets angry at petty things, the housewife who gets the blues, the businessman who hates to fail, the student who is confused, the grandmother who is afraid.

It deals with feelings, dreams, disappointments, and happiness. For sometimes happiness is as difficult to cope with as disaster.

It is not for deep-seated personality deformities—just for everyday problems that we all face sometimes; and sometimes we can get help from reading a book like this.

# 1

## Sometimes I Am Afraid

As human beings we all belong to the same large club called
the Fraternity of Fear. Despite our age or occupation, even the
calmest of us suffers from some form of worry, anxiety, or
insecurity. There are extreme cases of people who refuse to
leave their room or stand from a wheelchair merely because of
fear; but the majority of us fall into that wide class of "normal"
*Homo sapiens* who fight the common fears of life.

Unfortunately, Christians who have less to fear than others
are often among those who are the most afraid. It is neither
practical nor desirable for Christians to erase all their fear.
Nor should they feel guilty because they are not as brave as
Tarzan or as bold as a circus barker. God has not intended to
make us fearless (despite some of the testimonies we hear), but
certainly he is willing to free us from destructive and
debilitating phobias.

Some fear is good and should be treated as a tender com-
panion. The person who boasts that nothing bothers him is
like a little boy whistling in the dark to prove his courage.
There are dangers in this life, such as snakes, crooks, drunken
drivers, and tornadoes, which give all of us the willies
sometimes. God built into us warning bells and lights to

protect us and we should have no desire to have all of them disconnected. A good healthy fear of God is not a bad concept either and probably needs to be shared by more people.

The type of fear which is most harmful to us is the kind that has no foundation in fact. The type that plays on our imagination or conjures up potential tragedies that are unrealistic. How many people spend large amounts of time worrying about their jobs and yet are never fired? Even of those who actually are "canned," 95 percent report that they found a better position while the other 5 percent claim they have one just as good (*Nation's Business*, November 1967). One person reported that he was always afraid of meeting a certain person around town. He knew that this gentleman hated him and was spreading rumors about his character. When finally forced to meet him at a party he was shattered to discover that the stranger did not know his name or who he was. There is a great deal of unfounded fretting and worthless worry.

The Christian who lives at this level is like the man walking across the nation while his wife drives the car. He will still make it but it is going to be a very uncomfortable trip.

Happiness is too often missing from this type of person. The word *worry* comes from an old usage meaning to choke or to strangle. Fear seems to have that effect and tightens up the individual and deprives him of enjoying the great pleasure and freedom of living.

How vital can our testimony be to the non-Christian if he assesses us as being afraid all of the time? The very things he tries to offer to others he does not have himself. Would Christ have been very inviting to us if we pictured him as a tense, uncertain worrywart?

The physical dangers of living in continuous fear are often

repeated and well known by all. However, how many of us realize that maybe the reason we do not feel well and are fatigued day after day is because we are being drained by fear? We do not have an ulcer or a twitch but we are just fagged out most of the time. Learning to handle fear may be an important practical step toward feeling a great deal better.

There are many Christians who have a strong desire to serve Jesus Christ but they find themselves frozen by fear. They cannot bring themselves to face that class, meet their neighbor, or launch across the ocean. Their heart is in the right place and their intentions are beautiful but they remain immovable.

Possibly the greatest loss in the fear struggle is that the Christian has bruised his fellowship with God. He finds it difficult to communicate and often impossible to find any comfort or reassurance from his Lord.

A short tour of some of the problems caused by fear convinces us quickly that something must be done to help the situation. Fortunately there is definite hope for every Christian, and that help can start immediately.

First there is logical help. Most Christians are not mentally ill to the extent of being irrational or psychotic. They have merely talked themselves into being afraid and now they need to reason themselves out of it. One fine Christian mother woke her husband in the night because she was afraid. She had begun to worry about her son and whether or not he would be killed in the war. The illogic of it all was that the son was only four years old. She did not need a professional counselor or clergyman. She only needed her husband to reassure her that in fifteen years the war would probably be over and it was a little early to be afraid. The mother then went back to sleep, reassured.

Jesus Christ understood and used this approach to

alleviating fear. "Consider the lilies of the field." They do not stay up late at night worrying whether or not there is going to be dew in the morning. He says, "Think it through." If the flowers are taken care of, you will be also (Matt. 6:28–30). Do not buy trouble by trying to figure out tomorrow. Most of those fears are unfounded and illogical.

Another solution to fear can be called the operational approach. We are often afraid of things merely because we do not face them. One person was afraid to fill out his income-tax form. He just knew that he owed the government a great deal of money so he put it off until the last minute. Then, to his surprise, he found that the government actually owed him money. The weeks of anxiety and fear could easily have been resolved if he had simply faced the problem. His solution rested in doing something rather than worrying about it.

Most of us have found this principle to be true. Facing the problem is almost always easier than anticipating it. Even if it does not turn out pleasantly it is still better than all the wringing of hands that preceded it.

Some Christians balk at this point and believe that God must remove the fear and that they should do nothing but wait for him to sweep across them. However, action is not unspiritual, and we are responsible for our use of the resources that God has given us.

Nevertheless, there is a spiritual solution to fear and it is used too seldom. God gives us many promises in the Scripture which we need to incorporate into our lives. Dr. S. I McMillen once wrote that the best prescription a person can be given for fear and anxiety is Psalm 23. It can be taken with each meal and every night. God's promises are uncomplicated and very direct. We can do anything if God wants us to do it

(Phil. 4:13). He has promised to reduce our fear because he is here to help us (Isa. 41:13).

Yet promises such as these fall on cold hearts because a great many Christians fail to recognize an important feature about God: He really does love us. Many Christians say that on the cross God loved them but, daily, he is angry and short-tempered with all our failings. If this were God we would have reason to fear. But since he loves us all the time (Rom. 8:38, 39), he understands what we face in life. He does not add to our fears but removes them. We really know that he can and will handle it all.

# 2

## *Sometimes I Am a Failure*

A young, ambitious husband comes walking from his parked car toward his house. It is the end of a long day and you can tell from his sagging shoulders and bent head that things have not gone well for him in the fascinating world of business.

His wife flashes him a spirited "Hi, honey!" but receives only a grunt in return. He throws his paper down, kicks the child's rocker that is out of place, and sinks gruffly into his overstuffed recliner.

The day has been a bust. A large department store called and said they were dropping their sizable account and were not at all satisfied with his service. He failed big, and it hurts.

What does a Christian do when he faces failure in life? Is it possible to enjoy God on the days we strike out as well as when we hit home runs?

When we really fail big there are certain Christian concepts that we should remember.

1. God is the God of failure. He is the God of broken hearts and not just of laughter. Of injured bodies and not just of health. Of old age and not just of youth.

2. Thank God for failure. It is difficult to thank God for all things but it will prevent us from becoming bitter and angry at life.

3. Ask God to teach us something. If we do not profit from failure then it is a waste. It is hard to beat a person who can turn failure into gain.

There is no need to fool ourselves; winning is beautiful. The Christian attitude is not to aim at losing or to glorify failure as better than victory. When someone passes us the ball, we do not intentionally drop it because failure is better. But neither do we fear failure as though God were not in it.

David had a heart like God's, but David's growth did not come solely by winning. He also learned some tremendous things by losing. C. S. Lewis said that every story of conversion is the story of a blessed defeat.

If we have not failed recently, we probably will at some point. When we do, it may help us to take a look at Paul and at what he gained from failing.

Paul was a successful person. God gave him a lot of good things in life including special revelations that no one else had. God gave him a vision of heaven, allowed him to write one-half of the New Testament, and made him a special apostle with peculiar authority.

But there are a lot of risks involved in being successful. Paul might puff up like a frog and become swell-headed, begin to consider himself taller, a little better than the average Christian. Maybe a bit arrogant, a mite independent, just a little unrealistic.

So God decided to do something to help Paul. He decided to send some failure into his life.

We usually think of failure as being the sinister work of Satan, but this is not always the case. II Corinthians 12:7 says that a thorn was given to Paul to keep him humble. Satan may have done the work but God had the idea and simply unleashed Satan to accomplish it.

If God wanted to he could prevent us from ever failing. He could build a protective cushion around us that could not be penetrated. But God is too wise to do that. Suppose someone does not prepare for the Sunday school class he is teaching. God may bless the class anyway. But he may also do the teacher a favor by letting him look like an idiot some Sunday, just to get him studying again.

Failure comes as a gift of God. God allowed Satan to buffet Paul. The word *buffet* comes from the Greek word for knuckles. Satan gave Paul a punch in the mouth. It was painful and it had a purpose. Paul learned something in his failure. Failure was his friend. In failure he grew and became strong.

Failure is the opportunity to grow. When you talk to someone who has loved and lost, you see a tragedy. But, if you meet someone who has loved, lost, and learned, there is something beautiful about him.

Thor Heyerdahl thought he could cross the Atlantic Ocean with six other men on a papyrus reed boat. He set sail to demonstrate that Egyptians could have landed in South America centuries ago. As he came close to completing the journey the craft started coming apart and the men found themselves holding onto a shattered boat in the middle of a storm, and they had to be rescued.

The famous adventurer learned from his failure, planned a second expedition, and carried it through with ease.

How many times do we ask for a closer walk with Christ? Then God agrees to draw us closer and he puts us in the hospital for two weeks so we will trust him. The first day is fine, the second day is a little edgy, and the third day we want to strangle the nurse . . .

Failure is the opportunity to bring glory to Christ. Our ego does not fall gently and yet it has to take a back seat to Christ. Make an uncomplicated deal with God if you can. Tell God, "Lord, when I stand in front of that group Sunday I want people to see you. If falling on my face, stuttering, forgetting my notes will cause people to see you, I am ready. Pull the rug out. I am not trying to gather praise for myself." The person who can tell God that cannot lose.

Paul said in essence, "I have been kicked around a lot. People have called me names, I have gone without things, crowds have turned on me, I have been shipwrecked. But I take a great deal of pleasure in these things." Why? Because Christ was being glorified in Paul's infirmities.

Dr. Robert Mounce has written in *Eternity* magazine that a willingness to fail opens all sorts of exciting possibilities. If we are always afraid to fail then we are not willing to take risks. A medical doctor places a tract rack in his office. He takes a chance. Possibly patients will be offended and his business will go down. He knows that and does it anyway. He is not afraid to fail because he knows that Christ can be glorified even if his business decreases. His personal success is not the goal.

Count your failures. Name them one by one and it may really surprise you what the Lord has done.

Take the fear out of failure by giving it to Christ. It may open up a whole new concept: the joy in failure.

# 3

## Sometimes I Get the Blues

Everybody gets the blues sometimes. Life is not a continuous climb to new mountain peaks, always ascending to new and exciting adventures. It is not even a flat plateau of evenness and dependability. Life is a series of ups and downs that eventually leave us with the blues.

Over twenty years ago a young country blues singer named Hank Williams died in the back seat of a chauffeur-driven Cadillac. Alcohol had ruined his liver and heart at twenty-nine. During the two decades since his death he continues to be so popular that his estate has earned five million dollars, and almost thirty of his record albums are still on the market.

Part of his appeal is that he sang and wrote some of the saddest and loneliest songs ever heard. Titles like "I'm So Lonesome I Could Cry" and "May You Never Be Alone Like Me." When he sang the blues, millions cried along with him because they were just as lonely.

The Bible offers some concrete steps on how to fight the blues successfully. However, this remedy is based on the fact that the person *wants* to fight them. Many people enjoy discouragement and like to feel sorry for themselves. If a person wants to lock his door and suck his thumb, then probably no one will stop him. But when we are determined to fight the blues, the Bible comes to our rescue.

When discouragement gets us down it is our problem and we are obligated to do something about it. That does not sound very religious: man helping himself. To demonstrate that God expects us to fight that blue feeling, consider how he handled Job. Most of us think that Job had a right to sing the blues. He lost his family, his property, his health, everything. Did God cry with Job or wrap his arm around him? No! God said, "Gird up thy loins like a man, I demand of thee" (Job 38:3). Literally he said, "Sit up, pull in your stomach, wipe that frown off your face. Are you going to sit there and pout about your past or are you going to get on with life?"

Many people can keep the blues as long as they want. When they decide to dig out of that hole, things will begin to happen.

How did God treat Jesus Christ? Christ struggled with the devil for forty days and nights. After Christ won the battle the angels came and ministered to him. Where in the world were they during the battle? God wanted Christ to fight and to win.

Someone asked famous baseball pitcher Cy Young how he won so many games, 511 all told. The Hall of Famer told Norman Vincent Peale that back in those days they did not use relief pitchers. So he knew that if he was going to win he would have to do it himself. No one was going to do it for him.

God is not very likely to break down our door and come charging in to rescue us from the blues.

The Bible records the confidence of Paul when he said, "I can do all things through Christ which strengthens me" (Phil. 4:13). Christ does not promise that he will do all things but, rather, gives us the ability to do all things.

Paul wrote a letter to a discouraged young man named Timothy (I Tim. 4:12f.). Paul told him to stick in there and not let people get him down. Be an example, he said, keep on teaching, use your gifts but do not let people tie you up with the blues.

It is a lonely business, these blues. Even in a crowd the person is convinced that he is alone and that no one really understands his problems.

Sometimes this is the fact. When a young lady decides to give the ring back to her fiancé she can talk to all of her friends and relatives about it, but the lonely moment of decision is hers alone. She almost has to feel blue.

At that moment she needs to know one of the most important verses in the Bible, I Peter 5:7. The verse says: "He cares for you." It guarantees that you are never alone and that someone always cares: after the game when you dropped the ball; when the meal you cooked came out terrible; when your son let you down.

When the blues start to fill a room like fog—blinding and choking you—thank God that he stays in the room with you. The psalmist wrote, "Let my mouth be filled with thy praise and with thy honor all the day" (Ps. 71:8).

David, the warrior king, once got himself into a discouraging dilemma. While he was leading his army on an expedition, the Amalekites attacked Ziklag and carried off the women and children, including relatives of David. David returned to find the city burned, his own family carried off, the soldiers weeping, and the people talking about stoning him.

David became distressed as he felt all sides pressing in on him. He had no place to go to shake off the blues, but the Bible tells us he "encouraged himself in the Lord" (I Sam. 30:6). "Why art thou cast down, O my soul? And why art thou disquieted in me? Hope thou in God" (Ps. 42:5).

Feeling sorry for ourselves is very unhealthy. We often start to exaggerate our problems. Like a speck of dirt on a white shoe, they are all we can see. Certainly our problems hurt. Certainly we can see no way out of them. But usually they are not as bad as those many other people face. Maybe it would help to take out a pad of paper and write down the initials of all the people whose problems we would not want. Wouldn't it soon become clear that our problems are not the worst on record, nor are they unbearable.

Then, because we are Christians, we need to go and visit the people on that list. They are the ones who need their day interrupted, to be reminded that someone cares.

An effective way for us to fight the blues is to drop our problems and go help someone with theirs. We need to buoy up a brother. I Thessalonians 5:14 tells us to "encourage the fainthearted."

For those who are determined by God's grace to fight the feeling, there is a day-by-day deliverance from the blues.

# 4

## Sometimes I Lust

"Boy, is she a good-looking doll!" Those aren't very strange words unless they come from the lips of a pastor. One day while walking from room to room on hospital chaplaincy, after we had just left the room of a bright-eyed young blonde with the soft voice of southern gentleness, the pastor turned to me and remarked how gorgeous she was. The words nearly sent me into shock.

Pastors are not supposed to think such things, let alone say them.

As I thought about the incident, the real hypocrisy of it began to come home to me. I was thinking the same thing that pastor was, only I felt ashamed to say it. A famous Christian psychiatrist has said that we all play at this game. It is normal and natural for practically all men from all callings in life to look at and admire women. The real question is whether or not this is in fact a sin.

One senses the feelings of bewilderment and guilt if he tries to discuss this subject with an adult Sunday school class. As one young man put it, "You are afraid to open your mouth and admit that this is the way you think. Afraid that you might be the only Christian who thinks this way, or afraid that after you admit how you think, the other men will turn pious and refuse to admit that they think the same way."

Christian men treat the subject like an uncle who was a bootlegger; we would just rather not talk about it. But we must talk about it, otherwise we cannot decide if it is a sin and we cannot help each other to lead righteous Christian lives.

The problem becomes embarrassing when one reads the words of Jesus Christ, "But I say unto you that whosoever looketh on a woman to lust after her hath committed adultery with her already in his heart" (Matt. 5:28). A professional counselor announced recently on the radio that such teaching was ridiculous and produced unreasonable guilt. The genuine Christian cannot dismiss the words of Christ so easily. And yet the question is, how can he live with them?

You are sitting in a chaise lounge on the beach when suddenly you feel a jabbing elbow in your ribs. Immediately you know that your wife has caught you staring at the trim little blonde wading in the surf. Just what are you thinking? Does it qualify as lust and hence adultery?

James 1:14–15 can probably be a great help with this personal conflict: "But every man is tempted, when he is drawn away of his own lust, and enticed. Then when lust hath conceived, it bringeth forth sin; when it is finished, bringeth forth death."

Let me suggest that there are four stages to girl-watching: (1) Look and walk on. (2) Look and be tempted. (3) Look and want her. (4) Look and then have her.

1. *Look and walk on.* There are many men who simply look at a woman and actually admire her in a platonic sense. She is a lovely woman. They do not want her and they do not succumb to imaginary fantasies. In no way can this be labeled a sin. It does not even qualify as a valid temptation and is not included in this progression which James gives. There are many other men who find this level often impossible to maintain.

2. *Look and be tempted.* When a man looks at a woman and allows his mind to wonder and wander, he is being tempted. At this point he has not surrendered to temptation, he is merely being beckoned. He is saying in effect, "This woman could appeal to me sensually." If she could not appeal to him then indeed she is not even a temptation. At this point a huge screaming red alarm should go off in his head and he should directly drop his thought and turn his head. Shut it off. Think about something else. Divert the route of his attention. To this man goes the victory of having overcome temptation.

3. *Look and want her.* This is the stage that James says lust has "conceived." Jesus has taught us that this stage should not take place because we have at this point sinned in our hearts. To look at a woman and allow yourselves to think of why we want her or what we want to do with her is the conception of sin even though it has not given birth to the outward action of sin. Every conscientious Christian must be concerned to avoid this stage.

4. *Look and then have her.* This is the final act of having physically acquired the woman and engaged in obvious sin. Too many people have found themselves at this fourth step without even realizing what has happened to them. It began innocently and the person was unable to hold himself in check.

For the Christian who is willing to take these passages seriously there are some guidelines that he should bear in mind which may prove helpful.

1. *Do not quit.* The first reaction of some is, "Well, if God rejects people for lusting, there isn't any hope for me." Indeed none of us is worthy of the grace of God but still he has given it to us. Accept it. God saved me in spite of what I think and even do. The only alternative is that no one is saved.

2. *Avoid traps.* The person who comes home from work at

10:00 P.M., eats cold leftovers, and then has a fight with his wife is in for a bad time. It would be very easy for him to watch a torch singer on television and wonder how she could comfort him. The physical and mental have more influence on the spiritual than we often admit. If you doubt it, read I Corinthians 7:5.

3. *Foster self-discipline.* A person can go a long way toward disciplining his own mind. His first concern must be that he wants to resist this temptation. If he does not care whether he falls or not, there can be little hope of overcoming. The prerequisite to this is that he be concerned with what Christ thinks of him and not consider the Bible as just a book of good advice, something which many Christians seem to do.

In order to treat the subject fairly we must also include a plea for tolerance. Not for ourselves but for others. There are those who will read this and treat it lightly. Because you are not tempted to lust after women, maybe you do not appreciate the struggle other men face. Yet, for many men this is a daily battle, and these men need the prayers and sympathy of all; certainly they need no one's flippant condemnation.

# 5

## Sometimes I Feel Guilty

Guilt is a very strong feeling which hurts many thousands of Christians. Some are physically sick with insomnia, or even visibly shaken merely because their conscience is restless. Others are depressed or discouraged or moody simply because they feel that God holds some grudge against them.

Whatever the problem behind these feelings of anguish, we can be sure of one thing. God does not want us to feel guilty. The uneasy mind or nagging fear is not God's goal for the Christian. "And the peace of God, which passeth all understanding, shall keep your hearts and minds through Christ Jesus" (Phil. 4:7).

One young man told the tragic truth when he said, "I was a lot happier before I became a Christian." He had heard and accepted the message that we are all sinners, but he had not yet accepted the full forgiveness of God. There are some very definite steps which a Christian can take to erase the guilt feeling from his life and be set free.

The first important step is to distinguish false guilt from true guilt. Many believers are beating themselves over sins they have never committed. Socrates said that the unexamined life is not worth living. But we should remember that the overexamined life is not worth living. Advice comes from all directions on how to live for God: Do this. Don't do that. So much advice comes that if a Christian listened to all of it he would be torn apart.

Bill Bright, president of Campus Crusade for Christ, told the story of how he read missionary biographies and learned of some Christians who arose at 4:00 A.M. for hours of devotions. Bright tried it but it did not work. Then it dawned on him that those missionaries had no electricity and were going to bed at 8:00 P.M. He was trying to keep someone else's standards but out of their context and feeling guilty about it.

Paul was concerned about this type of Christian experience when he wrote to the Galatians. He said, "Are you so foolish? Having begun in the Spirit, are you now made perfect by the flesh?" (Gal. 3:3). There are many people waiting to tell us that we are guilty of sins that the Bible does not describe as sins.

A husband with six children one day heard a sermon on tithing. The minister insisted that Christians should tithe their time to the local church, and immediately this parishioner felt convicted. Some simple mathematics tells us that there are 168 hours in a week. This man attempted to spend seventeen hours a week or two and one-half hours every day inside the church. His family soon felt abandoned and the Christian felt thoroughly frustrated and guilty.

The happy Christian must avoid the pseudostandards which men impose. There are two steps that will help. First, allow the clear teaching of the Bible to convict your heart. Second, allow the Holy Spirit to convict you. These two are dependable, while the convictions of men are sure to lead to confusion.

If we feel guilty and the guilt is real, there are certain positive steps we as Christians can take to free ourselves.

We begin by factually recognizing our guilt, noting specifics rather than vague generalities. It is one thing to agree with Isaiah that we are "undone" (6:1–7) but just a broad confusion may not remove the guilt. If we have lied then we should say so. If we have cheated, stolen, hated, or whatever, let us admit it.

Sometimes we are embarrassed or reluctant to say, even to God, what our sins are. Yet the burden lifts when we know we have been honest and specific.

After we have faced up to what we have done, we may have to make restitution. It is impossible to be forgiven for stealing a library book if we then continue to keep the volume. In order for guilt to be released the book must go back.

Zacchaeus seems to recognize this principle in the Bible. After he ate and talked with Christ the tax collector announced that he was giving half of his wealth to the poor and if he had cheated anyone he would restore it fourfold. Then Christ announced: "This day is salvation come to this house" (Luke 19:9).

Receiving the forgiveness of God is not completed simply by identifying sin and making amends for the wrong done. For the Christian it also involves the confession of sin as described in I John 1:9. Confession is not begging or agonizing with God. There is no uncertainty about whether God will forgive. All we do is to agree with what God says about sin. God is saddened by it, disgusted with it. If we are fed up with that sin and feel the same way about it then automatically the giant eraser removes it from the chalkboard.

Some Christians are dismayed to find that confession does not guarantee perfection. They have confessed, only to find themselves sinning and having to come back again.

When a young boy had difficulty seeing well he was given

glasses to wear, with the promise "If you wear these while you are young you won't have to wear them when you grow up." He placed great confidence in this old saw and waited for the day. When he was twenty years old he was back at the eye doctor's for another adjustment. He asked the doctor, "How much longer will I have to wear these glasses?" The examiner looked at the young man and said very hard words, "You will have to wear them the rest of your life. You will always be dependent on glasses."

How long will we have to confess our sins? All of our lives we will be dependent on the cross for forgiveness and fellowship with God. We will always have to go back, but there is freedom for the person who will.

After we have dealt with our real guilt we need to take that extra step and accept the love of God. Jesus told us, "As the Father hath loved me, so have I loved you; continue ye in my love" (John 15:9). God is not angry at us. We should not imagine a cold, stern stare from God looking at the back of our necks.

There are some people who suffer from real neurotic problems who never seem to accept the love of God. They should realize that how they "feel" has nothing to do with fact. If we have confessed our sins we do have fellowship with God. Even before that the Bible tells us, "But God commendeth his love toward us in that, while we were yet sinners, Christ died for us" (Rom. 5:8).

Mark, chapter 10, tells us the story of the rich young ruler. Christ talked to this man who was about to reject him, this man who could not part with his wealth in order to follow Christ. This passage says (vs. 21) that while Christ talked to him he looked at the young man and loved him.

Jesus did not die so we could still shoulder the burden of our guilt. If we know the truth the truth will set us free. Joy and not gloom is the lot of the forgiven Christian. If God will forget our sins (Heb. 8:12) then why should we remember them?

# 6

## Sometimes I Can't Pray

It looks easy enough. When we watch a baseball game we think anyone could pitch one of those things. Just grab that ball firmly, wheel back, and throw it. If you want it to wiggle or dance around you merely move a few fingers around.

However, if you try to pitch you soon discover how hard it is to get the little monster over the plate, and if you are successful they knock it right past your head.

Throwing a baseball can be pretty discouraging, and trying to pray can be just as difficult. In fact, it can be so tough that one survey of a group of ministers showed that only one-third of the ministers prayed daily.

Yet the tremendous potential in prayer makes the practice worth cultivating. What prayer can do for the participant and the strength of prayer across the miles make it the most powerful and the most helpful influence in the universe.

If prayer has become boring, burdensome, and unsatisfying, possibly a look at the attitudes and teachings of Christ can give us a fresh new incentive.

Christ taught us that too many people make a mistake by praying to please men (Matt. 5:5–6). How long we pray, when we pray, and what we pray for is often dictated by the pressures of men.

Consequently we often pray in strange ways when other people are around. Instead of a simple prayer, we become very official, wordy, and rambling. Sometimes our tone of voice is more suited to the telling of ghost stories than to talking to God. What is normally a swift table grace becomes an excerpt from Calvin's *Institutes* when we have company.

Possibly we would be less afraid to pray if we considered prayer as talking to God. With a hundred people surrounding us it can still be just one person talking to one person. Christ is concerned that if we pray to impress people we will in fact pray *to* people. If we do, we can hardly expect God to answer prayers that are not addressed to him. Freedom in prayer comes as the individual is able to rise above what humans expect of him; it allows the communicator to seek the face of God boldly.

In order for prayer to be effective it has to be sincere rather than routine. Jesus Christ talked about men who prayed a great deal, and he called these men of prayer hypocrites. Their motives are wrong. They are self-centered and in fact insensitive to God.

Often we regard prayer as the pinnacle of the spiritual experience. The person who prays much must be a giant in faith. Yet, how do we explain the person who prays often and treats his family terribly? The one who prays regularly and mistreats people?

Without a humbled heart, without a willing spirit, prayer can become a license for a person to do anything and then look back and say, "Well, it must be okay, I prayed about it." Prayer cannot be a camouflage to cover up our mistakes. Merely to conquer the mechanics of prayer without a bowed heart will make prayer dangerous.

For prayer to be rich and rewarding Jesus told us to avoid empty repetition (Matt. 6:7–8). The word *garrulous* would describe much unhappy, fruitless praying. It means rambling, tedious, pointless, annoying.

Some hapless souls repeat the same three phrases day in and day out. God is great, Thank you for the food, and Bless the missionaries. Other prayers are wordy, measured by the yard rather than by sincerity. Some are surveys of Old Testament history: "As you were with Abraham on Mt. Moriah, Joseph in the pit, Moses on Mt. Pisgah, Joshua at Jericho, Ruth in the fields of Boaz." As the gentleman in *Fiddler on the Roof* asked while praying, "Why am I telling you what the Good Book says?"

In modern times prayer has taken on a very rigid form. Close your eyes, fold your hands, bow your head, now God will listen. While this approach has been very helpful in improving our concentration, it has also resulted in much sleeping, daydreaming, and runny noses.

We find people in the Bible praying in all assortments of postures and temperaments. They pray standing up, flat on the ground, head bowed between their knees, hands up in the air (I Tim. 2:8), and sometimes crying and tearing at their clothes. Others adopted a Tarzan style and beat on their chests.

For many their praying was not a dull stereotype and hardly an empty exercise. Possibly prayer would find a new vitality for us if we accepted our freedom and made some changes in our approach to prayer. More people are using short sentence prayers—even in groups. There is a movement toward conversational prayer. Removing the "thous" and "thines" and resorting to just talking to God. Opening our eyes might add a stimulus. Silence in prayer and just listening for the guidance of God may be a source of strength that is seldom touched.

Among those who are disillusioned with prayer there seems

to be the nagging guilt of how long to pray. We read of a spiritual warrior who spends an hour each day in dedicated prayer. This may be very admirable of the gentleman and certainly should not be belittled. However, it is really necessary to try to match his experience?

If two minutes in prayer is as long as you can concentrate, then pray for that long. You may later lengthen the time, and then again maybe you will keep it brief. Frequent short prayers during the day could be excellent. Any alternative is better than saying, "I can't pray for thirty minutes, so why bother?"

There is a lesson to be learned in the length of the Lord's Prayer—possibly the ideal prayer and certainly the one Christ gave his disciples as a model. How long does it take to say that prayer? I timed it and it took thirty-five seconds. There were times when Christ prayed for long periods, but in the Sermon on the Mount this prayer took only thirty-five seconds. The sermon he gave covers three full chapters, and yet the prayer is half a minute.

Someone has well said that good prayer is like good bacon, lean and meaty.

There are many keys to effective prayer. In the Lord's Prayer Christ ends by mentioning one of the most important keys. He tells us that our effectiveness with God in prayer depends in large part on our effectiveness with people. God's communication with us is somewhat contingent on our communication with others.

Christ said, "Forgive us our debts as we forgive our debtors." Later he said, "If you forgive not men their trespasses, neither will your Father forgive your trespasses" (Matt. 6:15). The person who is holding a grudge against his neighbor will find prayer a dry hole. The person who mistreats his wife will find the gates difficult to open (I Pet. 3:7). The person who is angry at being passed over for a promotion is seriously limited.

Prayer is the faith at its best. We talk to a God whom we do not see. We praise him, simply trusting that he will accept it. We send up a petition merely believing that he will answer.

By removing the cobwebs and dusting off a few shelves it would be easy for the smallest faith to grab hold of prayer.

# 7

## Sometimes I Doubt

While fielding questions during a Wednesday night service a minister very honestly remarked, "Sometimes I doubt there is a God." The response of the people ran from hostility to gentle consent.

Some in the group considered the statement outrageous and unthinkable coming from their pastor. A few insisted that they had never doubted the existence of God. Others were very sympathetic because the same shadows of uncertainty had crossed their minds.

Three cheers for those who never doubt; it must be a great way to live. Yet for those who are sometimes haunted by periods of serious questioning there should be some help and reassurance. To begin with, they are part of a large fellowship and by no means isolated or peculiar. The Christian psychiatrist Paul Tournier has said that, contrary to what we imagine, the greatest of believers are attacked by doubts.

Doubters also need to know that there is definite help for those who want to grow in faith. There is little assistance available for those who revel in suspicion. Pilate asked, "What is truth?" but he did not want an answer. Consequently, he remained unenlightened. Occasionally we meet the person who thoroughly enjoys his skepticism. He knows all the problems, he sees all the angles, he twists around all the alternatives like a gymnast on his horse. Doubt can be a healthy process through which we travel, but doubt is ugly if it becomes the goal of life.

In his book *Why I Am a Christian* (Minneapolis: Augsburg Publishing House, 1930), O. Hallesby says that doubt is better than dead traditional Christianity. He feels that much of the faith that existed in the Bible was of little value because it was impersonal. Instead of ignoring our doubts or surrendering to them, maybe we can benefit by exploring doubts and setting them to work for us.

One of the main causes for doubt is almost too simple to accept. Many people plunge into spiritual despair because they are physically exhausted. That may seem difficult to admit, but we cannot dissect ourselves into neat compartments of body, soul, spirit, and mind. The composite person is so tightly knit that one section must affect the others. Worry can give us ulcers or colitis. Prayer can raise us to physical fortitude or even to healing. If these components are interdependent, is it so absurd to believe that physical lows can cause a spiritual collapse?

How many people doubt their ability, their future, and their God at two o'clock in the morning? They are sleepy, hungry, and sapped of rationality. Is it surprising that such a person becomes despondent?

William Cowper (1731–1800) was an accomplished writer who often succumbed to depression and he attempted suicide before he became a Christian. After his conversion he still experienced many mental fluctuations; at some times he was strong and stable, other times he was weak and moody. Through these recurring clouds he managed to be an excellent poet and to write several notable hymns, including "There Is a Fountain Filled with Blood."

Some days Cowper did not feel like a Christian, but nevertheless he knew that Christ died for him. The sign of a struggle may not indicate a calamity but, rather, may signal the existence of life.

Elijah was a great prophet who had such faith that he could call on God and fire would come down from heaven. One day, after several spiritual "highs," he sat under a juniper tree feeling sorry for himself. He told God in essence, "I am rotten, why don't you just let me die?"

God could have responded in rage and chewed out his servant. He could have delivered a discourse on apologetics or outlined the doctrine of faith. Instead God knew immediately what Elijah needed. He told the prophet that he needed three things: some bread to eat, water to drink, and a good nap. When Elijah woke up God could use him again. (Read I Kings 19:4-8).

The next time we feel our tent is about to fold, it might help to look up at God and make an honest confession: "God, I am in a lousy mood today, help my faith until it passes." Then do something about it. Eat a sandwich, take a walk, or go to bed. It will do wonders for your faith.

There are other times when we see our faith gutted by the circumstances of life. While we might like to think that faith is not altered by events, that is very often the case.

A young man with a very pragmatic attitude toward God put it this way; "I am going to ask a girl to marry me. If she says Yes, then I will believe there is a God. If she says No, I will know that God is a hoax." Most of us hesitate to be this brazen, but we often are tempted to be.

When things go well for us, God is very creditable. When the winds are heavy, he seems a little more remote. We pick up a newspaper and read about a cyclone claiming thousands of lives and we wonder where God was. We lose our job or our health fails and it occurs to us that maybe God is asleep.

Before we conclude that we are odd for being this fickle, we should look at some other people who suffered from the same lapses. We once had an old friend named John the Baptist who had tremendous faith. He could point at Jesus Christ and say without hesitation, "Look, the Lamb of God" (John 1:36). Yet, later, when John was arrested and awaiting possible execution, he sent a message to Jesus and asked him, "Are you the one who was to come, or should we expect someone else?" (Matt. 11:3).

John believed, but the circumstances of life were hard on him and he wanted a little reassurance for his faith. Trials and disappointments are among the certainties of life. When they start moving in we do not need to think that God has moved out.

In her excellent book *The Hiding Place* (Old Tappan, N.J.: Fleming H. Revell Co., 1974), Corrie ten Boom tells of a Jewish Christian certain that he would be arrested and incarcerated in a Nazi concentration camp. He explained to his friends that while he did not know what would happen to him he did know that some people were going to hear about Jesus Christ. That is an indefatigable faith. A faith which cannot be fatigued or worn down or tired out.

My old friend Job said about God, "Though he would slay me yet would I trust him" (Job 13:15 LIVING BIBLE). Circumstances are temporary, but God is eternal. After the smoke has cleared and waves have calmed down, one immovable force remains. Hopefully wrestling with difficulties will only cause us to believe yet more.

For Christians who choose to confront their doubt and fight, Christ gives some great promises. He told us that if we choose the route of faith we can even have the power to cast mountains into the sea (Matt. 17:20). It is worthwhile to have this fantastic source of power in our lives, and here are some simple suggestions to help fight off doubts.

Read the Bible regularly. For us to listen to what everyone else says and writes and yet ignore Christ is being unfair to ourselves. Talk shows are deluged with tinsel philosophers —movie stars and comedians waxing eloquent about God ethics, and eternity. They have every right to express their opinions, but we hurt ourselves if we give them a better hearing than we give Christ. "Consequently, faith comes from hearing the message, and the message is heard through the word of Christ" (Rom. 10:17).

A second step in building muscles of faith is to surround ourselves with dependable Christian friends. Paul Tournier has said that loneliness often feeds our doubts. For most of us loneliness is an all-around enemy. God's very practical suggestion is that we cannot afford to stop getting together, in small groups, in congregations, or on a one-to-one basis. Without Christian friends faith is tough. "Let us not give up meeting together, as some are in the habit of doing, but let us encourage one another—and all the more as you see the Day approaching" (Heb. 10:25).

A third exercise in faith is to start serving others in the name of Christ. Faith is fragile if it is only an internal debate. Faith is its healthiest when it is lived out in the traffic of life.

Push-up number four is to start talking to God, not for long periods of time but in short sentences often during the day. Accept God as a personal friend rather than as a theological polemic.

Stand before God without any sophistication and unabashedly say, "Lord, I believe but I have trouble believing. Help me to overcome my doubts with simple trust." Those of us who have trouble with the doubt route fall into a large fraternity and God loves each one of us very much. Our motto is "I do believe; help me overcome my unbelief!" (Mark 9:24).

# 8

## Sometimes I Am Criticized

There are three ways a person can be criticized: for doing what is right; for doing what is wrong; and for doing nothing. We cannot choose whether or not we will be criticized because there are no "ifs" about it. We are left only to choose "how" we are to be criticized, not "if." Since it is going to come anyway, we might as well do what is right and take it on the chin with a smile.

William Wilberforce lived in England during the last century (1759–1833) and helped lead the fight against slavery. Because he elected to champion a noble cause for humanity, many people became heated in their opposition and began to spread false rumors about him. They claimed he beat his wife and otherwise abused her. They whispered tales of a secret marriage to a Negress.

As a Christian with a cause the options open to him were few. He could abandon his fight for freedom, but that would only alter the criticism and not erase it. He could retaliate against those who slandered him, but then he would become like them. Or he could ignore them and boldly get on with the job at hand.

Certainly the first step in handling criticism is to accept it as an inevitable fact of life. Many times we are hurt deeply by slander because we do not think it should happen. Then the arrow pierces our heart and immediately we cry "unfair," "dirty deal." A giant leap to maturity is to face the inescapable fact.

There is a gentleman in Kansas who seemingly gets along with everyone. Consequently someone feeling himself mistreated by friends sought counsel from this man with the winning personality. Surprisingly, the man replied, "I realize that God has given me the gift of getting along with people. But, frankly, there are some people who just hate my guts."

While all of us would like to be Mr. Nice Guy, it is not very realistic. Every normal caution should be taken to avoid being abused; however, if we try too hard we will sack our convictions, become indecisive, and end up knee-deep in contempt from everyone.

We would be safe in saying that the Bible does not tell us how to evade criticism. It only teaches us how to face it. Jesus Christ, the world's leading authority on being abused, told us what attitude would be most helpful when the walls come caving in: "But I say unto you, Love your enemies, bless them that curse you, do good to them that hate you, and pray for them which despitefully use you, and persecute you" (Matt. 5:44).

Certainly it is not natural, but then Christ did not teach us to do what comes naturally. Most of us would like to pray that God will give our nasty cousin a pimple on his nose. Or we would like to see a sweep of power that might send a plague of bedbugs to the whispering neighbor. Yet, Christ will not let us get away with that. It is not good for our adversary and it is not good for us.

David Livingstone emerges from history as a mammoth character—giant in adventure, giant in courage, and giant in faith. While he mapped Africa people attacked him verbally from every side. They said he was not a Christian, not a missionary, that he hated his wife and family. His reply to this criticism can give us an enormous boost: "I like to hear that some abuse me now, and say that I am no Christian. Many good things were said of me which I did not deserve, and I feared them. I shall read every word I can on the other side, and that will prove a sedative to what I was forced to hear of an opposite tendency."

Doubtless it was as difficult for Wilberforce and Livingstone at times as it is for us. Nevertheless, they tried to set Christian power into action by following the healthy teaching of Jesus Christ.

The person who spoke the words of Matthew 5:44 was both God and man. We have to be very careful not to rob Christ of his manhood. He was tempted in every way we are tempted (Heb. 4:15). Christ was factually criticized and abused, and it hurt. People spread rumors that Jesus was a drunk and a glutton. He decided not to run the rumor-mongers down or lie about them in return. Soldiers smacked him across the face and spat on him. He decided not to wipe them out.

Christ had the courage to take his teachings into the laboratory of life and try them out. Consequently he was able to teach us. When someone strikes you on the face, turn your cheek and give him another crack at it.

The next time someone starts to attack you and tear your reputation apart, you might benefit by asking yourself some helpful questions.

1. Is it true? If someone is telling all the neighbors that you have a still in your basement and you do have one, instead of going into a rage you should go downstairs and dismantle the still. It is cruel of people to attack you but it is an equal shame if you do not correct an admittedly foul situation.

2. Must justice be insisted upon? If you are attacked is it

only right that you head for your opponent's jugular because he deserves it and it will teach him a lesson? Christ says No, love him and teach him a real lesson.

When Christ was smeared he did not smear in return. We can be sure that when we say, "I am going to get him for that," we have stepped out of the safety of God's laws. God says that vengeance belongs to God and not to man.

Hitler had a lot of problems and one of his major ones was that he had to get even. As he went charging into World War II a sick passion kept driving him. He had to pay back the Allies for humiliating Germany in World War I. He was going to teach them a lesson if it took millions of lives to do it.

Paul's example could serve us well when we are tempted to tie a past score: "But this one thing I do, forgetting those things which are behind, and reaching forth unto those things which are before" (Phil. 3:13).

3. Do we actively show love to those who criticize us? It is said that when Secretary of Interior Walter Hickel published a letter criticizing President Nixon he received an interesting phone call from the White House. He was informed that he was not invited to the Sunday services that week at 1600 Pennsylvania Avenue. A senator from Connecticut criticized the administration and was told that it would now take his constituents thirty days to get passes to the White House. Normally it took a few hours.

Christ taught us that it is easy to love the people who love us—our children, parents, sweetheart. But then even the Pharisees do that. The real freedom in Christian love is to love those who do not love us.

A rubber band cannot snap back unless it is uptight. Christ would have us relax and take criticism with a healthy smile. Let us bless those that persecute and curse us (Matt. 5:44).

# 9

## Sometimes I Get Angry

A young man sits alone. A few minutes ago he told his friend—rightly—just where to get off. Now if only he could enjoy this moment! Instead, his stomach is churning with a sense of guilt.

This problem is not an unfamiliar one for the Christian. He has heard conflicting arguments on the subject, ranging from "It's never right to get angry" to "Remember, Jesus cleansed the Temple." A believer who wants to channel his emotions in the service of God should look again at the Bible's teachings about anger.

First of all remember that when you feel mad you are in no sense abnormal. Anger is a universal emotion. The person who says he never gets angry may need to ask himself some serious questions. Does the absence of anger mean he just doesn't care about life; or does he have an inadequate definition of this form of passion? Another thing you should consider is that the Bible seems to find anger can be either good or evil.

But the major portion of scriptural teaching is that the Christian should control and avoid anger. The word originally was associated with the picture of a plant that swells with juice. (In short, remember that when you are angry you may be making a sap of yourself!) The primary question to the believer ought not to be, "How do I let off steam?" but rather, "How do I prevent steam from building up?"

Let us put some Bible passages together and see if your anger is good or bad.

*A. Good anger:* Possibly the best gauge to use here is to ask yourself if your anger will serve God. Be careful how you answer this one.

One day Jesus walked into a synagogue and saw a man with a withered hand. The crowd around him fixed their eyes on him to see if he would heal on the Sabbath. The Bible says he looked around at them in anger (Mark 3:5). Our Lord was angry because these people had put their personal laws above compassion.

In John 2, Jesus cleansed the Temple. It is difficult to imagine him doing so in any mood but anger. In Matthew 23 he issued withering woes to the Pharisees.

If we take these three sections as illustrations, we can make these observations about a justifiably angry man:

1. *He knows why he is angry.* When we fly off the handle at frustrations we aren't using anger as Christ did.

2. *He does not defend his personal pride.* Christ did not react to having his toes stepped on by lurching out in counterattacks. His enemies felt his love.

3. *He is not getting even for wrongs done.* Christ taught that vengeance belongs to God.

4. *He is not rubbing salt into wounds.* Christ did not grow angry when he saw weakness in others. An understanding of this simple truth could prevent us from going into tirades against our children, mates, or friends.

*B. Evil Anger:* As we consider unjustified anger, we first look at Christ's example and then ask ourselves:

1. *Is my anger selfish?* The prophet Jonah suffered from feeling sorry for himself. Somehow he could no longer see the needs of others and his eyes became fixed on himself. He became angry because a plant died and in so doing deprived him of a little physical comfort. Yet there was a whole city dying without saving faith—and Jonah could not seem to get angry about that. Selfishness discolors. We sulk and in crushed pride we erupt in anger. Something may be wrong in the heart that gives birth to such feelings.

2. *Must others do it my way?* A close cousin to selfishness is the attitude that we cannot stand to have people disagree with us.

Jesus Christ was confronted in John 7 with people angry enough to kill him. He stood before his enemies and explained their problem to them. They were not really upset because he healed a man. They were angry because of the way he was healed. Jesus did not do it their way.

These types of anger are nonconstructive, dishonoring to God, and quite bluntly, an expression of the carnal man.

Honesty must admit that there is a good anger. But hostility is a dangerous emotion and every man must tread lightly. We need to be reminded of Jesus' words, "But I say unto you, that every one who is angry with his brother shall be in danger of the judgment" (Matt. 5:22).

Consider these five suggested attitudes:

1. *Avoid anger.* Colossians 3:8 says that we are to put off a number of attitudes, the first of which is anger.

2. *Go slowly.* James 1:19–20 gives us a better formula than counting to ten: (*a*) Be quick to listen. Make sure you understand what is being said. (2) Be slow to speak. Who knows, you may not have to say anything. (3) Be slow to show wrath. Be molasses in January at getting angry.

3. *Control your temper.* A person is in serious trouble if he cannot control his temper. Anyone with a low boiling point is a poor receptacle for Christian grace. To have the meekness of Christ means a believer cannot "shoot from the hip." Is this not the reason God told us not to select a bishop who was "soon angry" (Tit. 1:7)?

4. *Do not nurse anger.* If you find yourself angry, whether you feel it is justified or not, do not let it hang on. Once it is over, forget it. Ephesians 4:26 says, "Let not the sun go down upon your wrath." Let it run only a short course and then give it the coup de grace, or it could grow out of proportion.

5. *Do not let anger lead to sin.* When a Christian feels his "righteous indignation" he is liable to be overwhelmed with a sense of nobility. "I am right and he is wrong." He may then become abusive and lord it over a person he is angry toward. Ephesians 4:26 says, "Be ye angry, and sin not." Even when anger may be good, do not let it go bad.

Isaac Newton concluded that in physics for every action there is an equal and opposite reaction. Anger is also capable of causing equal anger in others. A wise person dispenses anger sparingly, because it may cause someone to sin by responding to him with anger. Ephesians 6:4 says, "Provoke not your children to wrath." The person who freely plants love in place of anger may some day harvest joy.

# 10

## Sometimes I Hold Grudges

During the early part of World War II a group of American fliers called Doolittle's Raiders staged a daring air raid on Tokyo. Six of them were shot down and captured. The Japanese treated the men with extreme harshness. Two of them were executed as criminals rather than being held as prisoners of war. Four others were beaten and abused.

Some weeks later one of the four prisoners asked a guard for a Bible. They were given a Scripture portion which they read and reread. They memorized large sections of it. Strangely enough, they found themselves no longer hating the guards who had treated them so cruelly. The Word of God had filled them with forgiveness.

A Sunday school teacher said to a hundred college students, "Think for one minute whether you know of a single person toward whom you feel animosity." At the end of sixty seconds almost all the students had been able to think of someone toward whom they felt animosity. In group after group, Christians have made the same admission. A great many believers are unhappy simply because they have not learned to forgive.

Some people are actually worse off for going to church on

Sunday morning than if they had stayed home. This may sound strange, but think it over. Have you ever seen a person leave church fuming because he felt cross toward the pastor, or had had words with a deacon or an argument with the president of the Ladies Aid? Instead of experiencing the peace felt by those who have forgiven, he was in an unhealthy state of emotional turmoil.

Christ forgave on the cross. God forgives our sins. But somehow we cannot always find the spiritual strength to say in our hearts, "I hold nothing against So-and-so."

You can probably remember vividly the dry, parched-throat feeling that comes from holding a grudge against someone. When you see him coming down the street you want to cross to the other side to avoid him. When you hear his name mentioned, you may say nothing but you feel the anger swell up in your throat like rising yeast.

God does not want you to live this way. He wants you to face the other person with a completely open and honest heart—and be able to say, "Mister, I don't hold a thing in the world against you!"

The Bible offers some basic guidelines on forgiveness:

*What should you forgive?* Is there really anything you cannot forgive? Begin by thinking about Jesus Christ. What did he forgive? The people who spat on him and murdered him. Cheats, traitors, the morally degenerate, and many more. To this very day he continues to forgive alcoholics, harlots, murderers, thieves, and all other sinners who are willing to accept his grace.

Suppose someone has hated you, lied about you, and cheated you. The Spirit of the indwelling Christ will enable you to forgive.

*How often should you forgive?* What's the sense of

46

forgiving someone, you may ask, if he is going to turn around and offend me again? This is the frustration of dealing with an habitual scoundrel.

Jesus answered this question on at least two occasions. His answer to Peter was crisp and to the point: If you are sinned against seven times in one day, forgive seven times in one day (Luke 17:3-4). On another occasion our Lord went further and said we are to forgive seventy times seven, or 490 times (Matt. 18:22).

People ask if that number is to be taken literally. The best answer was suggested by a college student who said, "If you are counting, you aren't forgiving. We can't say, 'That was 471. Nineteen more and I hit him right in the chops.' " Such an attitude desecrates the word forgiveness.

It may seem impossible, but Christ definitely teaches us to be never-ending in our forgiveness.

*Who takes the initiative?* Both logically and biblically, only one person is responsible to be the first to forgive. That person has to be *you.*

Some Christians are too proud to bury their complaints and let their wounds heal, but Christ tells us that if a brother has something against us we should drop what we are doing and go to correct the problem. "Well, if he comes to me . . ." is a stalemate in a game no one can win.

*Remember that Christ forgives you.* Forgiveness ought to be a communicable disease, but usually it is localized and we keep it well under control. We are to forgive one another even as God, for Christ's sake, forgives us (Eph. 4:32).

There is depth to the forgiveness of God. He has erased cruel and heinous crimes against him—we have denied him, or misued the Bible to our personal advantage, or misrepresented him before men. His forgiveness has breadth, too. He has forgiven adultery, murder, drunkenness, and a variety of other offenses.

You will find it helpful occasionally to remember the many sins for which God has given you mercy instead of justice. Then, recalling what God has done for *you*, you will be less likely to act toward *others* in weak, watered-down forgiveness.

The Bible has definite promises for a Christian who freely and fully forgives those who offend him:

1. *Freedom to Worship.* If you are about to give an offering to God, said Jesus, and you remember that a fellow believer has something against you, you are to forget your gift and go to make things right with your offending brother (Matt. 5:23,24). Perhaps God is telling you to stuff that check back into your pocket, to close your hymnal and not sing, or to remain seated and not testify, until you are reconciled. Your worship will count when your heart has forgiven.

2. *Freedom to Pray.* When you find the prayer channel clogged up, ask yourself whether your relationship with men is making your prayers impotent. Jesus said, "When you stand praying, forgive!" (Mark 11:25). A man cannot expect to find open communication with God if he is mistreating his wife (I Pet. 3:7). To say you have a heart for God when you have no heart for men is far from Christlike.

3. *Freedom to Face All Men.* It is unhealthy and unholy to have personal enemies—to allow people's behavior and words to ulcerate you. It is unwholesome and unspiritual to admit that if you meet a certain person your blood will boil and your conscience will accuse you because of the unkind things you have thought about him. It really hurts when you attend the funeral of a person who in life you despised. Revenge belongs to God, not to men (Rom. 12:19). A forgiving Christian need never feel two-faced when he meets anyone.

*48*

4. *Forgiveness of Your Own Sins.* You cannot escape your own guilt until you have shown a forgiving spirit to others. As you pray for a holy and forgiven life, be careful that you have done for others what you are asking God to do for you. An unforgiving heart may be warning us that we have not yet received God's forgiveness (cf. Matt. 6:14–15).

Inability to forgive makes for a miserable person, but this is one misery no one need experience. God will give you, if you really want it, grace to forgive.

# 11

## Sometimes I Am Confused

When you rap with young Christians, often someone asks, "How can I know the will of God for my life?" That's not surprising. Young people are about to make some tremendous decisions concerning career, college, and marriage.

So how *can* you know? Consider another question. How do you know when you are in love? Maybe you were walking down the street when you saw that certain someone. Right away bells started to go off, sirens whistled and psychedelic colors flashed before your eyes, and you knew you were in love.

No. That may happen to some, but to most it is quite a different story.

More than likely you saw him in a crowd, you heard him talking and it stuck with you. You soon found yourself going out of your way to be near him. You found yourself thinking about him, even daydreaming, until one day you realized that it had happened. You were in love.

It may be that knowing the will of God works the same way as love. Granted, some people receive the will of God by a sudden flash, a bolt of lightning, or a voice from heaven. Peter, Paul, Philip, and many others did. But for most of us it is a gentle, slow process of God molding a mind and heart.

It is sad to see people miss God's plan because they are still waiting for thunder to crack and a rock to light up with the word "biochemistry" on it.

A second misconception going around is to assume wrongfully that if God directs you to do something he wants you to keep doing it forever. Some of the most successful fulltime Christian workers were first established as businessmen, lawyers, schoolteachers, or housewives. God could be directing in one area for two, four, six years and then, zap, tell you to do something else. Just because God gives you a versatile and varied career does not mean you are a quitter or lack dedication.

After serving as a missionary, David Livingstone went to work for the government. He was criticized greatly.. But Livingstone felt that one could not evangelize Africa unless it was first mapped. A change in careers is not necessarily a change in commitment.

Paul was a missionary, a teacher, a writer, an apostle, a relief worker, a tentmaker, and much more.

A third myth to be discarded is the feeling that God leads only perfect people. Too many young people are up to their necks in introspection. They develop complexes, think they are the dandruff of the world, and believe that God is not interested.

The people through whom God works have the same failures, temptations, passions, mistakes, and hangups as anyone else. It is doubtful that many young people have as much trouble as Peter did when Christ spoke to him after the resurrection. The big difference between those being led by God and the others is that one group has said, "I am willing."

Back to David Livingstone—this time as a young person. After completing his medical and theological training he took a pre-missions training course. Livingstone royally flunked it, but he didn't quit. He was willing to take the course over, and God found a way to use him.

Whether God wants you to be a lawyer, missionary, dentist, or housewife or to sell hotdogs in the Astrodome, there are some basic steps that you as a Christian might follow to discover the will of God.

First, ask yourself if you really want to know the will of God. A lot of people do not, and it is important to be honest with God. If you are not convinced that God knows what he is doing and that you can trust him to give you a happy life, then say so. Jonah did not believe it. He heard the will of God and said, "Thanks, but no thanks." Yet he was honest enough later to admit God's will would be best, and then God led him on.

Paul said, "I am ready not only to be imprisoned, but even to die at Jerusalem." He really wanted to know the will of God.

Second, get a good version of the Bible and start reading it. You aren't going to find the words *neurosurgeon*, *nuclear physicist*, or *elevator operator* in Scripture. But the simple truth is that unless you read the Bible you do not know how God feels, what he thinks, what he wants, or his sense of values. We say we want to follow God, when in fact we know very little about him. We need to begin to think like God, rather than to be saturated by what surrounds us.

Third, talk to God about it. How can you expect God to call you if you don't have the telephone hooked up? You cannot take the attitude that if God wants you he will call you. *He wants you.* Maybe you better give him a call.

Fourth, talk to other Christians about it. We all know dedicated Christians who have successfully discovered what God had planned for them. Feel free to ask them how God led in their lives. Most people are more than willing to share, and they may open up new ideas that would not otherwise occur to you.

Fifth, do you do what you already know? Following God does not merely consist of consulting God on those big decisions like marriage and college. All of us know of things that God wants us to do right now: camp counselor, youth group officer, summer missionary. The Bible tells us to help, to be good workers, to be examples, not to lie or have other gods, and much more. Do not merely daydream about following Christ tomorrow when you can begin today. Once you begin, at least you know you are moving in the right direction, and it will be much easier for God to guide you.

## 12

# Sometimes I Feel Useless

·Many kinds of gaps exist in some of our churches. We can add to the generation gap, the credibility gap, and the "God gap" something we might call the "layman gap." This gap consists in the large number of adults who do not actively participate in any Christian ministry whatsoever. Part of the reason for this layman lapse is that most Christians do not realize they have a spiritual gift and very few identify their gift.

If anyone doubts this void, a simple test is available. Merely ask a group of Christian adults to raise their hands if they know what gift they have. In most cases the lack of response will be impressive.

The remedy for the unconcerned layman may not be criticism or services of dedication. His problem may be very elementary and just twofold. He does not know what spiritual gifts are, and he does not know how to identify his particular gift. There are four things that a layman needs to know about spiritual gifts—who, what, why and how.

*Who receives spiritual gifts?* The most extensive discussion of the subject is found in I Corinthians 12. Paul says that every Christian is given a gift (vss. 7-11). These gifts are not restricted to professionals or clergymen. At least one gift if evidently distributed to each believer at the time of salvation.

However, as Charles C. Ryrie suggests in *Balancing the Christian Life* (Chicago: Moody Press, 1969), a person may very well be given more than one such ability. He may be both a teacher and a missionary or a counselor and an administrator. Paul could both evangelize the non-Christian and teach the believer. Barnabas could intercede for Paul, start churches, and also carry funds to feed the needy.

Verse 31 of the chapter urges that the better (or greater) gifts be desired. If there is no teacher for a group or situation, it would be proper to ask God for someone gifted in teaching to fill this need.

*What are spiritual gifts?* We must distinguish between spiritual gifts and talents. A spiritual gift is of supernatural origin; however, it is not the same as a natural talent. It must be conceded that if a person accepts Christ at an early age, it may be difficult to distinguish between a gift and a talent. Both gifts and talents can be used to help the local body of believers.

The fact that a gift has a supernatural stamp upon it does not mean that the gift is already developed. Training and experience are needed. God does not give the gift of teaching so that, without preparation, golden nuggets fall from one's lips. Countless people who have been used by God first received an education and then constantly prepared, studied, and practiced to use that gift effectively.

Fifteen years ago God used an excellent accordion player to reach many for Christ, both young and old. While in the Marine Corps he played a solo for President Eisenhower and Premier Khrushchev. He was very talented, but one reason for his skill was that he practiced six hours a day.

A spiritual gift needs to be developed by such helps as training classes, correspondence courses, books, and watching others practice it. God supplies the basic tool, but we need to learn how to use it well.

Possibly too many Christians are very limited in their concept of what a gift might be. Begin by looking at verses 8–10 and 28–30 of I Corinthians 12. Notice the many different types of gifts which the Spirit dispenses.

Gifts of "governments" (vs. 28) are gifts of administration. They may be evident in Sunday school superintendents, members of a Christian education board, college administrators, or mission executives.

One layman said, "I tried teaching Sunday school, but I just couldn't get the knack of it. Now I am the superintendent and I just love the job."

What is a gift of helps? This gift may be seen in a faithful worker in the missionary society or women's fellowship, in a children's home worker, or in a volunteer worker in a hospital. The doors for using such gifts swing wide and may open much broader opportunities than our vision has previously allowed.

*Why such gifts?* The answer to this question will help greatly in determining what our gifts may be. First Corinthians 12:7 says the purpose of gifts is "to profit"; it is for the common good. Ephesians 4:12 states the purpose as "for the perfecting of the saints, for the work of the ministry, for the edifying of the body of Christ."

Consequently, the best rule for identifying a spiritual gift is to ask whether or not it fulfills the purpose. Does it contribute to the body of Christ in some edifying and helpful way? If it does, then it certainly ought to be exercised.

When a Christian neglects a gift or refuses to discover what it is, the Church, the Body of Christ, suffers because part of the Body has ceased to function. Surely this is one of the reasons why the Body of Christ is weak. Many do not begin to use their gifts.

A correct appreciation for one's gift also will prevent an

enormous amount of jealousy. Unfortunately, some Christians sit around and boil over the fact that someone else was selected deacon or that another person is Sunday school superintendent. Such steaming is destructive energy.

*How does one find out?* The first step in doing this is to dispel two extreme feelings: a feeling of false modesty and a feeling of superiority. Many people do not want to admit they have a spiritual gift because it sounds immodest. Some also are afraid that if one should say she has a gift of teaching, another person will say, "She isn't such a good teacher."

Remember that a person who acknowledges a spiritual gift is not saying that he is a good teacher or even a better teacher than the one next to him. He is saying that God gave him a gift and to his class of five or fifty he will exercise that gift. He is the person whom God wants to use in that situation, and he trusts God to work through him. The word "gift" does not mean that one automatically is superior.

A second step toward discovering a spiritual gift is to consider why one wants to know if he has a gift. If a person is only half interested or has merely a "museum" curiosity, then he perhaps may not come to know that he has a particular gift. The person who wants to know for the purpose of using his gift is on the way to discovering it.

A third step is to gather information. The one seeking to find his spiritual gift should read these passages of Scripture mentioned and know some of the possibilities. Then he should talk to other Christians—the pastor, missionaries, the Christian service committee, some elderly believers, and other knowledgeable persons. They will probably alert him to possible avenues of service and offer some very helpful suggestions. The searcher also might be surprised to learn that he is already exercising his gift without knowing it.

A fourth step is for him to try some different avenues while asking God to reveal his gift. How many have said, "Why, I can't teach a class," and yet they have never tried to teach. Some say, "I can't work with elderly people," and they have never tried. If a person sits in a room and says, "I can't, I can't, I can't," then indeed he cannot; but if he searches and tries, he will discover what he can do.

God has given every Christian a gift. Happy, fulfilled Christians will find out what it is and use it.

# 13

## Sometimes I Am Lonely

After living in a large metropolitan apartment house for five years a man could frankly say, "I know no one on my floor and only one person in the entire building." Most people are not surprised to hear that in this insulated and isolated world so many people find it difficult to make friends. Indeed Billy Graham wrote some time ago in *Reader's Digest* that when he is asked what is the number one problem plaguing our people, his reply is, "Loneliness."

The present-day Christian can go far in helping people by simply reaching out to the lonely and becoming their friend for Christ's sake. Too many people walk out of a cold world and into a church seeking warmth, only to discover the identical blast of chill. There is a great opportunity for Christians to show sincere compassionate concern.

One young man said, "I walked into a church where I knew no one and there I received Christ as my Savior. In the same day I met two young Christian men who became my friends. They were responsible for keeping me interested and attending in the hard months ahead." There are many Christians who could give similar testimonies.

God recognized this need among Christians in Hebrews

10:25: "Not forsaking the assembling of ourselves together." If Christians have no other reason to get together, they must meet for the purpose of fellowship and encouragement. How many times has a Sunday school class or a sermon gone flat but still you were uplifted by the presence of other believers?

The local Christian church has all the resources necessary to wrap its arms around the lonely and the seeking that enter our buildings and neighborhoods. Yet at least two things often leave us icelike. First, because of the sizes of our churches many of us assume that George will take care of it. George will greet them, he will remember their name, invite them to Sunday school, take them home for coffee. Second, many of us are snug inside our security blanket of present friends and we dare not venture outside to pull anyone else aboard.

The process of cultivating friendships is, for the believer, necessary on many grounds. Making friends is a ministry to others and it also fills a need within our own lives.

Sometime travel through the Scriptures and try to realize the broad potential for the Christian who is willing to make new friends.

1. *Reach out for friends.* There are all kinds of people in this world who need good friends, just as you do. There is probably not a person you meet who would not be helped by receiving a sincere friend. The fact of the matter is there are more people who need your friendship than you could ever begin to handle. Proverbs 18:24 in essence, "How are you going to gather in friends? By paying the price of being friendly." By giving up selfishness long enough to share with other people. Friendships are not always convenient, but the person who will spend his time, consideration, and energy toward others will be a person with friends. Many people who have no friends have really never tried to be a friend. You are

not a flower waiting to be plucked by a passing friend. Take the initiative. Pick up your phone and invite someone to share an event with you.

A young man one day had two tickets to a football game. He thought of a young teenager, so he called him and took him to the game. That man never lacks for friends because he has proven himself friendly.

2. *Choose friends carefully.* There is a strange paradox in the Scripture, a knot we should try to untie. The Bible teaches that Jesus was a friend to publicans and sinners (Matt. 11:19). He walked among the ungodly without fear. He proved himself friendly and caused a number of sinners to believe in him. Yet, at the same time we know that it is dangerous to become too closely yoked with unbelievers (II Cor. 6:14). Indeed James 4:4 says that a friend of the world is an enemy of God. How, then, can we safely become the friend of an un- saved person?

Maybe the answer rests in a simple test. If in your friendship you can influence that person in the name of Christ, as Christ himself did, then fine. However, if the unsaved friend has more influence toward ungodliness than you have on him toward Christ, then possibly it is a friendship you cannot afford.

It is a risky business to walk into the camp of Satan and try to steal his people, but it can be done and should be. But do not be too proud to admit that a certain person is too difficult and too tempting for you to handle. Back off if necessary.

3. *Friendships can backfire.* Every person should enter into a friendship with his eyes wide open. Even with the best of friends, relationships do sometimes go sour and people do get hurt. This should not discourage us, and we should still become involved in people's lives. But do not become unduly

shocked if today's friend should become tomorrow's enemy. That is part of human nature and part of life. Still, friendships are a precious part of life and not to be avoided just because we could possibly get stung.

A Christian has to remember Jesus Christ and the harsh treatment he received. One day he was teaching the seventy disciples and preparing them to go out and preach in two's. Christ told them, among other things, to cast out demons. Mark 3:21 tells us that when Christ's friends heard this they turned against him and tried to seize him because they thought he was mad.

There will doubtless come the time when you must follow the leading of the Lord in your life despite the open disapproval of your friends. Yet, do not be discouraged. Friends are frail and capable of error, like everyone else. The wholesome benefit of nurturing friends far outweighs the possible damage.

4. *Help your friends.* Some teenagers asked a Young Life leader, "How come guys like you care about me and my gang?" Despite all the pale jokes about a "friend in need is . . ." it would still be a miserable friendship that did not offer help. There are many fibers that make up a friendship; among them are concern, trust, care, sharing, and help. Can he be your friend if you do not want to help him?

Jesus Christ performed a miracle in a man's life. He cast demons out of his body and the demons took up residence in some pigs which promptly ran off a cliff (Mark 5). Naturally the man was grateful, but far more than that he volunteered to become a missionary and follow Jesus Christ. But to the surprise of many of us, Christ turned down his application for foreign duty. Christ said, "Go home to thy friends and tell them how great things the Lord hath done for thee and hath had compassion on thee."

Cornelius demonstrates this attitude when he learns of Peter's pending arrival in Acts 10. Cornelius is not just caught up in the excitement of hearing the good news from Peter, he is not simply thinking of himself. Rather, verse 24 states, "And Cornelius waited for them, and had called his kinsmen and near friends." This is part of the evidence of a good friend.

Job went through disappointment and abuse at the hands of his friends, and yet at the end we still find this righteous man praying for those very friends (Job 42:10).

5. *Make God your friend*. Man will find no truer or closer friend in life than the intimate friendship that is possible with God himself. God becomes more than a Creator or a Judge, though he is all of that. God seems very much concerned to become man's personal friend. James 2:23 discusses Abraham and says that he believed, consequently God imputed righteousness to him and he was called the "Friend of God."

In friendship God wants to develop a relationship of trust, of sharing, of honesty, of frankness, of helpfulness. Not that God wants to become "Butch," your old buddy, but he wants to maintain a close warmth that makes you feel at home and causes you to know he cares.

Doubtless this was what Christ had in mind in John 15:15 when, looking at his disciples, he said, "Henceforth I call you not servants; for the servant knoweth not what his lord doeth; but I have called you friends. . . ."

What a friend we have in Jesus, and such a friend we ought to be to others.

# 14

## Sometimes I Am a Worrywart

Imagine that every evening a thirty-year-old man goes down into his basement to stand by his workbench. He then places his left hand into a vice and with his right hand tightens it until the pain becomes unbearable. For one hour he stands there and sweats in agony as the throbbing shoots up his arm and into his head.

If someone tortured himself this way every day we would not know whether to laugh at him or pity him. After all, self-torture is an odd, sad state of affairs.

And yet, every day countless Christians go through this same type of misery by the pitiful practice of worrying. The Greek word for *worry* comes from two words, meaning to divide and to mind. Literally it means to tear one's mind apart. One-half of our mind is here and now, while the other half is stretched into tomorrow. Consequently, the mind is strained and pressured out of shape.

What kind of oddball Christian worries anyway? The fringe Christian who only half believes? The lukewarm Christian who is wishy-washy? The facts are that some of the most respected Christians are prone to be worrywarts. Charles Spurgeon, the great preacher in England, used to worry so much about some speaking engagements that he wished he would have an accident or break a leg before the service.

David is such a fascinating character because he could be so noble and yet so ordinary. God promised David that he would reign on the throne of Israel. Yet, in spite of God's specific promise, David still worried that Saul might kill him.

Some people really prefer to worry. They are even sure that things will go badly if they do not fret. Fortunately for those who are not happy with worry, Jesus Christ probes the problem and shows us how to fix it. People have real problems and the teachings of Christ do not gloss over them.

Suppose a man has a broken leg, he is out of a job, and they have repossessed his car. Can we say to him, "Don't worry, everything will be okay"? That's not true; everything will not be okay. But worry will not help. Work, planning, a loan—all may help; in fact almost anything but worry will help.

Worry not only hurts, but also is counterproductive. It prevents us from making the most of *now*. A person cannot sleep because he worries about next week. Consequently today suffers. It inhibits us from thinking clearly, making decisions, or planning ahead because a divided mind leaves us with only half a mind to think.

What does worry really help? Suppose you are a teenage boy 5 feet 3 inches tall and you want to play professional basketball. There are only two things you can do about it. Smile or cry.

Smiling will not make you 6 feet 8 inches, but, Jesus said, neither will crying (Matt. 6:27). You can worry, become bitter, develop a complex, but you cannot grow eighteen inches by worrying about it. Worrying is useless.

Imagine all the terrible things that could happen tomorrow. You could break your foot or get fired. Your hair dryer might short circuit and burn off all your hair. Your chicken might die. Your two-year-old might throw up in the supermarket.

But to worry about any of them will not change them.

The birds have no stores, banks, cars, insurance policies, or irrigation systems. Yet a bird does not sit and sulk about life. A bird does not jump out of a redwood tree and kill himself (Matt. 6:26).

Worry wins the grand prize for being both useless and illogical.

There are a lot of people who worry their way through life because they think they are useless. Often they look in the mirror and recite all their miseries. "I am a dummy." "People don't like me." "I am going to flunk." "I have terminal dandruff." Jesus was a very practical teacher and pointed to the everyday things of life. He pointed at the little poppies of the field and told us not to worry (Matt. 6:28). God takes care of the flowers, so do not imagine he has abandoned us. If Jesus died on the cross for us, dare we imagine that we are worthless? Christ says our worries are irrational. They do not agree with the facts.

If God says, "I will leave you tomorrow" then we have something to worry about. But as long as he says, "I will never leave you nor forsake you," worry is irrational.

Simply agreeing that worry is useless and irrational does not cause it to dissipate. Christ goes beyond this diagnosis and prescribes two medicines to cure worry. (1) Seek first the kingdom of God; (2) live one day at a time (Matt. 6:33–34).

Worry is a pagan practice. The pagans do not know whether their gods will be with them tomorrow or not. They have something to worry about. When a Christian worries he is not a pagan, for most Christians worry. He is simply a Christian with a pagan practice.

Christ taught us, "Let not your heart be troubled." Why? "You believe in God, believe also in me" (John 14:1). Christ was being logical and rational: Since you believe in God and me, your heart does not have to be troubled.

66

When we visit with a seriously ill person it is not fair to say, "Don't worry, everything will be all right." We do not know if everything will be all right. But we can say, "Don't worry, God will be with you today, tomorrow, and forever."

To seek first the kingdom of God is to know Jesus Christ. Then we have the only guarantee about tomorrow—Jesus Christ will be with us.

As certainly as a person short-circuits his life by being haunted by the defeats of yesterday, so he hurts himself by courting the ghosts of tomorrow. Ghosts that have never appeared, ghosts that are as harmless as empty sheets, ghosts that may prove to be a mirage when tomorrow finally comes.

The only security we have for tomorrow is that we have found a place in the family of God and we are immovable from that fold (John 10:11–12).

# 15

## Sometimes I Feel Hopeless

Many people would not make very good seeds. A seed is planted in the ground and dirt is thrown over it and it just sits and waits. It cannot see in the darkness, it has no guarantee of water, and it cannot be sure it will ever see the sunshine again. It could just start to sulk, watch the worms crawl by, and eventually rot.

However, a seed has enough determination that no matter how dull the circumstances, it will begin to fight. Even if it is planted upside down it will turn around and make the tough struggle toward the top.

A great many people would not make very good seeds. If they are down and under, they calculate the obstacles and immediately conclude that everything is hopeless.

That is the same reason why the gospel of Christ does not help everyone. The gospel is really good news for dreamers: the person who dreams that there is a bright tomorrow, the person who dreams that the marriage wound can be healed, mothers who believe their son will find help, young men who believe they can be leaders in a world that needs them.

The New Testament tells a lot of stories about people who were not afraid to dream. A woman who had been sick for twelve years had a dream that if only she could touch Jesus

Christ she would be healed. After she touched him and was cured, Christ told her why it happened: "Daughter, your faith has healed you" (Mark 5:34).

More psychologists seem to be coming to the same conclusion. People are in search of hope, expectation, or the feeling that something good is going to happen. The gospel of Christ has that message and it needs to be taught positively to the many who need to know it.

Imagine a man sitting home late at night in his living room. The lights are low and everyone in bed. The sad look on his face tells you that he has troubles. The fact is that he is deeply in debt and his oldest son is on the verge of being expelled from school. For years he has heard "Prayer changes things" and "Christ is the answer." It is a fair question for him to ask if these sayings are empty or if he dare dream that they might be true.

The Bible is itself a book for dreamers. Why does it contain such a large collection of stories? Is it just an archive of Jewish history or a short life of a fascinating man named Jesus? Rather, it is a book of hope that relates not only how dreams come true but even things that people were afraid to dream.

As a case in point, look at Abraham. We find a man up against the impossible. God told him about a land, about a son, and about a nation that would all be his. Abraham had little reason to believe these things would happen except for a promise, and then Abraham started to dream. Maybe the promises of God really do come true, and he fixed his heart on these promises rather than on the obstacles. Romans 4:18 says, "Against all hope, Abraham in hope believed and so became the father of many nations, just as it had been said to him."

Many of us have never realized our dreams because we have been afraid to dream. If we never expect anything we will not be disappointed, so we keep our goals low in life. Consequently we not only do not achieve the impossible we often do not accomplish the possible. The man who does not believe he can be a leader is perfectly right. The father who does not believe he can communicate with his son is right. The girl who does not believe she can be a lawyer is on perfectly safe ground.

The war cry of the pessimist is, "It is always darkest just before it gets black." How many of us own the book of dreams, the Bible, and still believe that nothing will work? The United Nations is useless. The battle against inflation won't work. The political system cannot help. People are crooks and not to be trusted. Surely we cannot be content to be authorities on what will not work.

Job went through so many heartaches and losses that it is easy to see why he took out papers in the local pessimist club. With his skin covered with worms and blackness, his flesh broken open and full of pus, he said, "My life flies by—day after hopeless day" (Job 7:6 LIVING BIBLE).

Yet, from that dark side of life Job learned to live again and watched his world turn into light. From this misery Job rose up to say of God, "I know you can do anything and that no one can stop you" (42:2 LIVING BIBLE).

There is a story that during England's darkest hours of World War II, Winston Churchill met with his staff. He looked into the gloomy faces spaced around the table and said, "Gentlemen, I find it rather inspiring."

The answer to the question of the man we mentioned earlier begins with an "if." Does prayer change things? Is Christ the answer? Yes, *if* we are not afraid to dream, to imagine things we have never seen before, to picture life as it could be.

In 1968 Louis Russell saw no light at the end of his tunnel. At forty-three the Indianapolis schoolteacher's physical condition had become so poor that after dinner he would go immediately to bed and he would also remain there each weekend. Russell had no hope of living a normal life, or even surviving, unless he had a heart transplant.

After discussing it with his wife they both agreed. A new heart meant two things: a chance to live and a chance to share their faith in Jesus Christ. They saw a chance, a ray— a dream—and they continued in the dark tunnel with only faith that there was light at the other end.

While transplants may not be the answer for everyone, for the Russells it meant six more years of life, and Louis used it to the fullest. He worked with young people, spoke to as many as twenty audiences each month, and personally counseled many others. By putting his faith in Christ into gear and concentrating on the possibilities rather than the obstacles, Louis Russell received a valuable portion of life that pessimists would never know.

The book of dreams will help create a people of dreams. The very word *hope* means to expect something good tomorrow and it is possible to rearrange a person's thinking until he starts to look for the bright things. Some have learned from childhood to expect the worst in life. It is the feeling of "impending disaster." Even if things are going well, they are convinced that something terrible is going to happen. It is a gut feeling that is not based on circumstances. They simply feel that way most of the time.

It is almost as though some people have a mind that is slanted downhill. If a person puts anything in his brain it will naturally slide down and almost never up. As Proverbs 18:14 says, "A man's courage can sustain his broken body, but when courage dies, what hope is left?" (LIVING BIBLE).

Some have fought depression for years and they now think there is no hope for tomorrow. Abraham's experience reaches out and cheers us on. "Against all hope, Abraham in hope believed."

The apostles knew how to fail royally in their lives. They tried to heal a young epileptic but they just could not get the job done. Finally Christ did the job and the disciples were left puzzled. They complained, "We tried to heal him, what went wrong?"

Jesus explained their problem, "Because you have so little faith. I tell you the truth, if you have faith as small as a mustard seed, you can say to this mountain, 'Move from here to there' and it will move. Nothing will be impossible for you" (Matt. 17:20).

One step in hope is to dream. Make a list of the things you would like to see tomorrow. A mended marriage. A well child. The return of a prodigal. A sober father. To become a disciple of Jesus Christ. The sky is the limit as to what you put on the list, and you are hindered only by your inability to believe or dream. Very few things will happen unless first there is a dream.

A second step is to ask Christ to help make it come true. His promise was simple, direct, and challenging. "And I will do whatever you ask in my name, so that the Son may bring glory to the Father" (John 14:13). There are exceptions to this rule, but if we major on the exceptions we kick the hope out of tomorrow. Part of faith is taking Christ at his word.

A third step in hope is to persevere. If we are fickle about our desires, if we continuously switch tracks, if we are unsteady about our goal, then very few tomorrows will come true.

Maybe that is why Christ told us that if a man puts his hand to the plow he cannot look back. To be second-guessing ourselves is the road to indecision and disaster.

When we start to waver we might do well to recall the story (Mark 2) of the men who brought the sick man to Christ. First, they believed that Christ could do something. Second, they would not let the pressing crowd discourage them. Third, they were willing to tear out a roof. Fourth, they saw the man healed. If any of the first three had got them down—if they had run short of perseverance—the man would have remained sick.

A fourth step in hope is to remember that seeds do not stop and sulk or feel sorry for themselves. If they did there would be no flowers on earth.

There is hope for people who are not afraid to dream.

# 16

## Sometimes I Suffer

Pain hurts. Words, books, songs, and ancient poems do not take away the agony. The man lying in a hospital bed with a swollen infected leg is suffering and it will not be denied. The young child with an inflamed appendix and the grandmother with gnawing arthritis are experiencing real misery and it takes more than pretending to make it go away.

Few facets of life are more universal or more baffling than physical pain. Why does it happen? Does God cause it? Is it a form of punishment? Does the devil send it? Is it purely a natural act and part of the lot of man?

Life has been described well by the sage of antiquity, Job: "Man that is born of a woman is of a few days and full of trouble" (14:1 KJV). Some people have felt so much despair touch their families that they agree with Martin Luther who once concluded that it was easy to believe in the wrath and anger of God, but hard to believe in God's love.

In many ways God has taken a bum rap concerning pain. Continuously God is accused of causing heartaches and tragedies when he may be entirely innocent. While God is involved in pain and helps the sufferer he has not necessarily sent the pain.

To take a sane and biblical approach to physical pain, it will help us to look at different types of suffering and ask ourselves which kind we are facing. Automatically all of us are threatened by pending pain. We know we are going to receive pain if we continue to live. The only blanks to be filled in are when it will arrive and what form it will take. As long as life lasts, pain will remain in vogue and be worn by people of all varieties.

The only option open to us is how we choose to react to this inevitability. We can become morbid and anxious. We can worry about broken legs that never break or heart attacks that never attack. Many people are renting pains that they will never own.

Other people are waiting for pain while making heroic proclamations. "When pain comes, Christians should rejoice," or "Pain is just an opportunity to grow." It is difficult to take such philosophical idealism very seriously.

Nevertheless, if pain is not now trespassing into our lives it is a safe occasion to study the subject and search the Bible. One lady in the hospital remarked, "When you are sick it is hard to think rationally. That's when we have to rely on what we already believe."

When pain actually begins, it generally falls into one of three categories:

*Passional pain.* This is a noble pain and consequently easier to live with—when a person gives up a kidney for a relative or stays awake for a sick child or misses meals so he can share with the hungry. It is the pain of the volunteer.

*Purposeful pain.* One young man had so much work done on his teeth that he looked forward to receiving the needles that would numb his gums. An operation which removes gallstones is genuinely painful but it is a means to an end and consequently more bearable. Jesus explained such pain in one of the best-known texts in the Bible: "A woman giving birth to a child has pain because her time has come; but when her baby is born she forgets the anguish because of her joy that a child is born into the world" (John 16:21).

*Pointless pain.* By far the most difficult to live with is futile agony. The man who spends thirty-four years in a mental hospital suffers from a hopeless pain. When a twenty-six-year-old mother of five is killed, there are few words of comfort that will suffice. Some people may even reject God because neither answers nor assistance comes after long periods of wrestling and even begging.

It is very possible that in our attempts to scrutinize pain we are asking the wrong questions. The most difficult question to solve is "Why did this happen to me?" As a form of self-pity most answers to "Why?" are very unsatisfying. Maybe pain will become profitable when we can ask a more mature question by posing the challenge, "What now?"

Where do we go with this pain? Bitterness? Resignation? Rationalization? Blame? Or, rather than looking for a cause, can we ask how God can use our pain? Job looked for a cause for his tragedies; finally, instead of trying to fix blame, he gave his situation to God.

Since God is so resourceful and imaginative, if we dedicate our pain to him he will show us a way to use it.

The disciples ask the same question that every man is prone to ponder. Seeing a blind man they immediately ask, "Why?" Was he a sinner or were his parents sinners? (John 9:1-5). Christ's reply went directly to the "What now?" This man is blind so that the work of God can be displayed in his life. What was Jesus saying? The man was not blind because God was punishing him or his parents. But God could take the handicap and bring glory to God. It was a pointless despair until God transformed it into good.

Christ told the relatives of Lazarus the same thing concerning his sickness (John 11:4) which resulted in death. God can be glorified by what has interrupted his life.

Some writers on American Indian life feel that in several ways the tribal religions were far superior to Christianity. When disaster or early death afflicted their families, Indians did not try to delve into the mystery of "Why?" They accepted hardships as a natural part of life. Leaves fall, snows come, birds die and so do people. Rather than attributing special theological significance to every event in life, maybe we need to approach pain as an inevitable part of our existence.

A very gifted Christian hymn writer living in the midwest suffered from a number of physical setbacks. Eventually his condition worsened until he was almost completely paralyzed and needed continuous care. Nevertheless he pushed on with his writing ministry even when all he could do was dictate to a tape machine.

His loving wife finally broached the inevitable puzzle, "Honey, why must this happen to us?" His reply was crisp and realistic, "Why not us?"

The apostle Paul wrestled with the same torn soul and when the match was over he walked away the winner. The pain still existed but he learned to seek the grace of God rather than someone to blame (II Cor. 12:7–10).

To be perfectly candid there are occasions when God does cause people to suffer. Sometimes when we have wandered far into the darkness of sin God will call us back. If we do not come back God loves us enough to chastise us if necessary (Heb. 12:6–8). Consequently, a hospital bed makes a good chapel and crutches make an excellent altar. However, once we have searched our heart and dealt with our problem, we must move on. We cannot afford to wallow in morbid remorse.

In all probability God has not sent the pain, but even if he has we should now move on to gain the most benefit from our sickness (James 5:13-16).

All of us suffer from pending pain. It is going to happen unless a swift heart attack wisks us quickly away. When that pain begins to tear at our marrow, some promises from God need to be kept in mind.

1. Absolutely nothing can separate us from the love of God. The loneliness of pain will make us wonder if even God himself has abandoned us. The reassuring answer comes back that God does not forsake us (Rom. 8:35-39).

2. God is capable of meeting all our needs (Phil. 4:19). When it seems that we cannot possibly face tomorrow, how often have we found an added strength that we did not expect? It will be there again.

3. God promises that some day the curse of suffering will be lifted (Rom. 8:21-22). Then Christians will never suffer again (Rev. 21:4).

God still holds the handle on suffering. The person who is in pain and asks, "Lord, how can I use it to serve you, to help others, and to grow personally?" can make pain pay. Otherwise it is a desolate road.

# 17

## Sometimes I Am Stingy

One of the most powerful influences on the American people during the past twenty years has been a modern philosopher named Hugh Hefner. As a contemporary sage he has not been the author of large dusty volumes but, rather, the editor of a slick magazine called *Playboy*.

The doctrine which he teaches is an ancient one called hedonism. Very briefly, it teaches that the greatest goal in life is personal pleasure. The hedonist's motto could be "Never put off until tomorrow the fun you could have today." The result of their approach borders on stark selfishness.

At the other extreme in life is a pattern called asceticism. It teaches that pleasure is wrong, that the greatest joy in life is not having joy in life. Pleasure is sin, a good time is frivolous, and the great goals of life are hard work and the simple life.

In the middle of these two extremes is fixed a far better way of life called Christianity. It teaches that man should enjoy the reasonable pleasures of life without becoming unbalanced in either direction. Jesus Christ told us that he enjoyed life, and people criticized him for it. They called him a glutton and a drunkard (Matt. 11:19). Nevertheless, such slander did not force him to abandon his very sound position in life.

John Locke, the great mind behind the American Constitution, was a professing Christian. He felt that man had to be guaranteed the right to happiness because Christianity taught man to enjoy life. Eventually, we were issued the right to the pursuit of happiness.

Coupled with the encouragement to be happy is the balanced necessity to sacrifice in this life, to surrender some of our pleasures, to relinquish some of our rights, to distribute some of our goods to other people.

The Christ-centered approach to life is "Happiness coupled with sacrifice."

The word "sacrifice" sounds stuffy and a little scary. Maybe we picture ourselves stretched out on a torture rack about to be wretched in agony. Or else we see a vision of ourselves standing in rags outside a crumbling shack because we sacrificed. The fact is that there is nothing to fear in sound sacrifice. It is healthy, it is cleansing, it is helpful. The person who has learned to sacrifice for others knows that he has been part of the noble life; he avoids the dry taste of centering everything on himself.

Christ did not invite us to relinquish our leftovers in life. He did not tell us to sacrifice some of our spare time. He did not instruct us to serve others when we were in the mood. He wanted followers who were dedicated to the difficult, and in doing it find a greater essence to living.

The apostle Paul wrote to the church at Corinth and explained what made the people at Macedonia such good givers. "Out of their most severe trial, their overflowing joy and their extreme poverty well up in rich generosity. For I testify that they gave as much as they were able, and even beyond their ability. Entirely on their own, they urgently pleaded with us the privilege of sharing in this service to the saints" (II Cor. 8:2–4).

They were not restricted to giving what was excess at the end of the month or doing without a few luxuries. They actually gave "beyond their ability." This type of giving is of the highest order, a help to man and a praise to God.

Sometimes we treat God as a fast investment: If we give away $100 we expect him to send us $150. If this were the case, all of us would quickly give away all our goods in order to get back more. Sacrifice is not a good "deal," sacrifice is a good heart that is willing to loosen up and reach out because the love of God is flowing through the person.

One woman wanted to make giving a personal extension and involvement, so she chose to fast once a week for several months. Then she took the money she saved and gave it to a missionary couple.

In order to get the full fun from sharing with others, Christ gave us some guidelines and cautions. Christ told us to not brag about what we give and to avoid being a "sourpuss sacrificer."

We have all seen giant color posters of the sort that read "See Gomo the Colombian Gorilla. 27-inch biceps. Champion of the Amazon Swamp. Will wrestle three men while eating an ice cream cone." Old Gomo puts his physical prowess on display and everyone expects him to.

However, when it comes to giving for God there is no room for Gomo. To give so we can display our trophies is a violation of godliness. Imagine this scene in our society. The church service is calm and serene. The ushers are passing the plates with dignity and poise. All of a sudden a young man in the fifth row stands up, blows a trumpet, drops in $10, and sits down. Fortunately we have never seen anyone do that, and in all probability Christ did not either. When he talked about it he was merely making fun of the extremes that people go to in order to receive recognition when they sacrifice (Matt. 6:2).

In order for giving to be wholesome and at all satisfying it cannot be a game. Giving for prestige, giving for attention, giving for advantage is sacrifice of the foulest order. It is an exercise in selfishness and unacceptable in the Christian framework.

Certainly there is nothing wrong with feeling good about sacrificing. We have followed a higher instinct, we have responded to a nobler call, and without thought of personal gain we gave. It should make us feel satisfied and glad we were able to do it. Paul told his friends he appreciated their gifts because "They are a fragrant offering, an acceptable sacrifice, pleasing to God" (Phil. 4:18). A clear, open conscience should make us feel good.

## 18

# Sometimes I Lie

Every husband has been there one time or another. He is sitting in his favorite chair reading the paper when his wife walks into the room.

"Well, honey, how do you like it?" his wife sweetly asks as a smile sweeps across her face.

She is standing there in a brand-new dress. It is black, has a large red bow that ties at her middle and an ample orange flower graces the top.

At that moment the husband knows he is in trouble. She spent all day shopping, paid $45, and plans to wear it tonight. If he tells her the truth he knows she will cry and dinner will consist of leftovers.

While this may not appear to be the greatest problem to rattle the western hemisphere, people are confronted daily with the choice of whether or not to tell the truth. In our own household: to our children. On the national level: to the American people. In the business world: to consumer and merchant alike.

A member of the president's cabinet made a statement at a press conference on the economy. An alert reporter challenged the remark, "Sir, is this not the opposite of what you told us last week?" His astonishing reply was, "Yes, but if I had told you the truth then our program would not have worked."

With so much contradiction all around us, we have to wonder how important the truth really is. Can we say anything we want today, and tomorrow merely announce that the statement is now "inoperative"?

Caught in a cobweb of flimsy values, we have the right to ask if the truth really matters anymore or if it all depends on the circumstances. Most people have to make an honest choice sometime. Maybe it really would be better to tell a lie. Maybe the truth would do more harm than good. ·

In order to ferret out the facts, we need to find a consultant on morality whom we can trust. Naturally our search leads us back to Jesus Christ.

We soon find that Christ is very helpful concerning the problems of personal integrity. He teaches us that ethics are of great consequence in the God-controlled life. Too many people have learned to equate prayer, Bible reading, and church services with living Christian discipleship.

Once I spoke at a college camp about some very practical aspects of life and one girl complained, "I hope we aren't going to do this all weekend. I came here to get something spiritual." Is it really possible that our concept of God has degenerated to the place where we do not believe he is interested in how we talk and treat people?

Jesus helped us by giving us a dependable guideline. He said, "Simply let your 'yes' be 'yes' and your 'no' be 'no,' anything beyond this comes from the evil one" (Matt. 5:37). In short, we cannot afford to play around with truth. We cannot be sneaky about integrity, filled with half truths and creating suspicion rather than respect. Ecclesiastes put it this way: "It is far better not to say you will do something than to say you will and then not do it" (5:5 LIVING BIBLE).

At a very young age we learned to play games with the truth; some feel we were even born with the skill. As children we would claim, "I'll give it back, cross my heart and hope to die." Then later we explain that our fingers were crossed so it didn't really count.

Then we grew up and the games changed but they did not disappear. We promise to take our son to a ballgame, but the chance comes to work overtime so we just skip it. We are pinched for money one April, so we shave our income tax just enough to make it fit.

Jesus knew some fascinating people who played a sneaky game with morality. They would say, "I swear on the Temple that I will pay you back on June 1." December shadows would cover the Judean hills and no sight of the payment. When the creditors complained the Pharisees would merely say, "Oh, we swore by the Temple but we did not swear by the gold on the Temple, so it doesn't count."

These people were not three-year-olds hiding bottle caps. They were adults, and worse yet, they were the religious leaders of Israel. Christ taught us that our word is binding, oath or no oath. If we say we will, we will.

Otherwise there is no morality. Everyone is subject to the whims and fancy of the other person, and we become victims of that person's fickle code of life. It has long been difficult to cash a check in many of the larger urban areas; now even the rural sections are mounting signs which say NO CHECKS. In some sections the number of bad checks written increased 30 percent in one year. We are the victims of a cotton-rag code of ethics, without form or strength and manipulated to fit our personal tastes, moods, and expediencies.

While lying often appears to be an appealing alternative, in reality it only hurts everyone: children lying to their parents and parents lying to their children; citizens fooling their government and governments beguiling their constituency. Man must consciously vote for a Christian morality or he is doomed to mutual distrust and destined to be victimized by his fellow man. Paul told the church at Colossae that lying could not become the Christian's modus operandi. "Do not lie to each other, since you have taken off your old self with its practices" (Col. 3:9).

Many of the kindest people in the world fall into subtle traps which destroy their credibility. The plain fact of the matter is that most of us talk too much. Some of our most magnanimous plans get us into remarkable trouble. If a person says he is going to paint his house, we quickly volunteer and assure him that we will be there. If a person asks us to pray for him, our immediate response has to be Yes. Then we forget, and fail to keep our word.

Too often we feel that we need to be a cross between Santa Claus and Ronald McDonald. If there is anything we can do for anybody just let us know—you can count on us. Sometimes our efforts to befriend people end up as the shattered dreams of dishonesty because we were unable to keep our word. Promises need to be dispensed sparingly to be restricted to the realm of our ability. Well-meaning people can ruin things by overextending their generosity. We need to promise less and do more.

Once a man received a letter asking for a recommendation for a young person. He had filled out so many forms before that it had become merely routine. And yet his conscience bothered him. The person in question was not really qualified for the position and in his heart he felt he could not make a worse choice.

Now he had to wrestle with his own integrity. It would be easy to write a favorable recommendation. Everyone does that, and yet was it really honest? He finally wrote a frank report because he realized that kindness can distort truthfulness and positiveness can become a destructive lie. How many people have been injured because their friend could not carry the cargo of truth?

Throughout our personal history of fluid ethics we have made some serious mistakes. We have made promises only to find that we have overstated ourselves or the circumstances have changed. Often our friendship then becomes estranged. We may begin to avoid the person who trusted us. We might begin to lie in an attempt to cover up our original statements.

Life is too short to spend it in this quagmire of guilt, deception, and confusion. To live in the sunshine we may need to explain our situation to our friends and associates. Tell them why we cannot pay the bill. Describe what changes prevent us from keeping our promises. Admit that we exaggerated from the beginning. Hiding or fighting cannot be the solution to correcting our mistake. Many people could put down a heavy burden if they would only explain what had happened. Is there anything more important in life than our personal integrity?

A young teenager made a promise to God. If he could be used on the mission field he would dedicate his life and serve on foreign shores. The years went by, marriage came and three children followed. Now white was dotting his sideburns and still that promise of twenty-five years ago haunted him. Finally, a very troubled person, he stopped and talked it over with God. A strange peace immediately flooded his heart. God was not holding him to that promise and all of his fretting had been futile. If only he had been able to face the problem earlier, he could have had years of freedom and tranquility with himself and God.

Telling the truth is not always easy. However, we can all be encouraged that if we intend to do good we will find a good way to do it: "For a good man brings good out of the good stored up in him, and the evil man brings evil things out of the evil stored up in him" (Matt. 12:35).

# 19

## Sometimes I Am Unhappy

A few years ago I wrote an article for *Eternity* magazine titled "Heaven Will Be Fun." Not a very profound piece of literature, it merely outlined some of the biblical descriptions of what we might do in heaven. The reactions were mixed and intriguing. Some Christians actually objected to the concept of fun. They felt that fun belonged to Satan and a wicked world and not to God.

The very idea of being happy creates strange ambivalent emotions in many people. On the one hand, they want to reach out and grasp happiness and at the same time they feel ashamed for even wanting it. Is it true that God wants me to be happy or is life ordained as a long series of heartaches while I struggle on to find contentment only in the next world?

It would be easy to be cynical and imagine that everyone is a miserable cuss with a sour outlook; however, this is not the case. There are not many people saying, "Boy, would I like to be miserable. Kick me, hit me in the head. Set my ear on fire." No matter how old we become or restricted our circumstances, we would all like a fair dose of fun. In this search for happiness we find a cheerleader called the Bible urging us on and hoping we will come out the winner.

*The Living Bible*, paraphrased by Ken Taylor, gives us a refreshing and accurate translation of the Beatitudes (Matt. 5–7). Instead of the ancient "Blessed be the man" Taylor has written "Happy are those" who are pure, merciful, kind, and so forth. *Good News for Modern Man* translates it the same way.

Two concepts have to be established in our minds before we can discuss happiness. First, people have a normal right to be happy, and second, there are many genuinely happy people in this world.

It was always amusing to hear some people in the suburbs of Detroit remark on how unhappy the rich auto executives in Grosse Pointe must be. They might have been surprised to learn that the executives were happy as well as affluent. We must be careful not to judge other people by our own feelings. Happiness is a reality. It may be elusive, it may be difficult to define, but for some people in life it is at the core of their existence.

One industrial tycoon complained that her happiest years were the early days of her marriage and family. Granted her later years were sour, but she had known happiness and it is an attainable goal.

Where then are the rays of light and the fresh air called happiness? Which windows do we open? What mountains do we climb? Consider some suggestions that might prove helpful.

1. *Stop looking so hard for happiness.* A very prominent woman was once asked if she was happy. Without flinching she replied, "Yes." Then the inquirer asked, "How did you find it?" And her smiling answer was, "I stopped looking for it."

For the many people who are intensely grinding away

looking for happiness it will always escape them. The very intensity of the search makes it impossible to find. They are uptight about happiness and creating the antithesis of their goal.

Jesus Christ was happy and he never rode a double ferris wheel. He never ate a banana split or visited Disneyland. He never rode a minibike or scored four points in overtime. But Christ was happy. Unfortunately some people do not find the two concepts compatible—Christ and happiness—but maybe they have an inadequate view of both.

We are not suggesting that Christ frowned on pleasures. If he walked among men today our imagination can picture Christ water skiing, playing shortstop, and even eating cotton candy if his beard would allow it.

However, even without these aids, Christ managed to enjoy life. The race for happiness is never won. One sprint leads to another, one mountain leads to a higher one. We need to stop the frantic scramble for happiness and look in another direction. It is like the luckless young girl who wants to catch her handsome man. Often she is better off to stop hunting and become a restful trap. Then she can engulf him because she backed off.

2. *Get involved in the interest of others.* Part of the certain disaster of seeking happiness is that it is often a very selfish pursuit. While a certain amount of contentment and even excitement come from personal ambitions, a great deal more comes from being interested in other people.

Jesus Christ spoke to this point when he told us in essence to picture a large banquet room with all sorts of dignitaries in attendance. A famous football player, a campus queen, the governor of the state, a movie star, a wealthy industrialist, a minister. Now ask yourself who, you feel, is the most successful person at the dinner.

Christ said the greatest, most successful, happiest person at the banquet is the person serving the tables. That person found meaning to life because he was able to help other people (Luke 22:24–27).

It is easy to appreciate what Woodrow Wilson said to the graduating class at Swarthmore College. He was the product of a notable education, having earned a Ph.D. in political science, and was past president of Princeton University. When he addressed the class at commencement he told them frankly that he was not impressed. He was not impressed with their degrees and knowledge. We forget knowledge and knowledge even changes. He told them he would be impressed when he saw them reach down and help someone who was less fortunate than they were. When he saw honor and principle, he would believe they had received an education.

The important key to happiness was held by Christ. He could say the Son of Man "did not come to be served, but to serve, and to give his life a ransom for many" (Matt. 20:28). The great object of life is not to grab, get, or reach. The happy life is one spent on other people who need help.

The story of George Washington Carver is of immense value in sorting out values in life. Born a slave, he eventually took a pygmy peanut and a distorted sweet potato and became the father of synthetics. He made everything from mayonnaise and shampoo to bleach, plastics, and shoe polish from these humble products.

Once an industry asked Carver for some formulas for dye and reportedly enclosed a blank check for him to fill in. He mailed them more dyes than they requested and returned the check. He said, "How can I charge others for the gifts of God?" It is a remarkable life that wants to contribute and distribute rather than merely collect.

Part of the cultural revolution and rejection of a few years ago was exactly this. People were discovering that happiness could not be founded on self-centeredness. In one college town where we worked it was great to see students going to the local rest home and "adopting" grandparents. Visiting them regularly and brightening their day because they saw life as an opportunity to give of themselves rather than just a giant rip-off of the world around them. It is to understand the words of the happy Christ when he said, "For whoever wants to save his life will lose it, but whoever loses his life for me will find it" (Matt. 16:25).

A lot of people are bored with life because they are bored with themselves. They have stood on one foot and then the other, accumulated amusement after amusement, and still they have missed the essential ingredient. They never learned to be big spenders—to spend themselves on the people and the world around them.

3. *Be diversified.* Some people do not enjoy life because they are in a rut. They work too much, or they play too much or they may even help other people too much. What could be unhappier in life than to develop an unbalanced pattern?

An evening in a restaurant with a friend is a good thing. Buying new furniture can brighten someone's outlook. A nice vacation might make a person enjoy his home more. The diversions of life are helpful and often necessary to the total picture. As long as no part of life becomes overwhelming to the exclusion of the other parts.

Solomon was healthy, wealthy, and wise. He wrote that

there was a proper time for everything. A time to plant, harvest, rebuild, repair, gather stones, and a time to hug, love, dance, and laugh (Eccles. 3:1–8).

Christ said a lot of strange things and some of them concerned achieving happiness in life. If we go about it correctly we have every God-given right to be happy.

"I am come that they may have life and have it to the full" (John 10:10).

# 20

## Sometimes I Am Tempted

How many times have we felt thoroughly ashamed of ourselves? We told a lie to one of the children, we spread some juicy gossip about our neighbor, or maybe we even pocketed a few dollars that were not clearly ours.

Afterward we award ourselves the "bonehead" trophy for distinguished stupidity. We often want to do our best and yet it seems so easy to foul up and do something lousy. Getting disgusted doesn't seem to solve anything because before long we find that we have done something else equally hideous.

A man once said he had this same problem of constantly falling on his nose. He put it into words and in so doing spoke for all of mankind. "I do not know what I am doing. For what I want to do I do not do, but what I hate I do." (Rom. 7:15).

Certainly there must be an answer to our natural gravitation to doing wrong. There has to be hope that somehow we could do better. Paul was the man who wrote about our condition in the verse we just quoted and the wise apostle was able to find a solution to his dilemma. When he wrote to the church at Corinth he gave them an outline on how to tie up temptation, and we need to consult his plan (I Cor. 10:13).

*Step One*: Remember that everyone faces temptation. While the first step may seem elementary, it is nevertheless vital to finding victory. Some people are convinced that they are the scum of society. As one person put it, "If my friends knew what I think they wouldn't have anything to do with me." The fact is that we might all be surprised to discover how closely we each think alike.

Consequently we cannot give up before we even start. We are all related both by birth and by natural inclination.

So, welcome to the club. We can't afford to feel sorry for ourselves, because self-pity is our deadly enemy. There are no immunization shots against temptation so we are far better off if we learn how to cope.

And yet there is something comforting about the fact we are all birds of a feather. We know the type of struggle our friends are going through in their daily lives and we know it is not easy. Consequently we are slow to condemn someone else because we honestly identify with them and know they have a heavy load to carry.

Even people we might look up to and respect are going through the same struggles. A minister told a group that he received $200 in cash in the mail anonymously for his church. Not being overpaid the thought occurred to him, "Who would really know if I only put $100 in the plate?"

To receive a fast course in human nature we would do well to read over Hebrews 11 again. It contains a list of distinguished people who were famous for the faith— Abraham, Isaac, Jacob, Sarah, Joseph, Gideon, Samson, David. While we read that chapter we might recall all of the evil that was committed by these ancient heroes. How many times did they face temptation only to be clubbed over the head and shanghaied.

Temptation is a very careful tailor. It tries to suit our personality. While everyone is tempted we are not all tempted the same way. Temptations are aimed at our particular weakness.

Some people could never be tempted by drunkenness because the very thought seems repulsive. Consequently, a little cash is flashed before their eyes. Possibly others could never be tempted to use drugs, so Satan will tempt them to gloat over their appearance or athletic prowess.

Sometimes we think, "Why, she is a fool to be jealous over another girl." But we must remember that if she is a fool she may only be a different type of fool from what we often are. Satan will start to work us over. He may grab a hold on our foul temper. He may start to scratch our itchy palm. He may begin to control our roving eye. He may pull the lever on our quick tongue.

We are not so different from others and we have learned not to be swift to get down on a friend who is stumbling around.

*Step two*: God is in control. We need to picture a very loving God looking at us and personally guaranteeing us that temptation will not overpower us so that we cannot handle it.

We can think of God as a gigantic, immovable rock where we can tie an anchor. Throughout our temptation God does not forsake us even if we go under.

The coal miners have a code which says that if there is a tragedy in the mine the rescue workers will not stop searching until they have retrieved everyone. That is faithfulness. When temptation starts to swallow us and it becomes dark and stormy and we begin to sink, the words of I Corinthians 10:13 come back: "Who will not allow you to be tempted above that you are able."

God has promised to hold the temptation down. God sets

up a security guard over our life. This is not a fantasy. God will personally see to it that no temptation enters our lives which we cannot handle or resist.

No monster will arise from a misty lagoon and steal us away at night. No chilly voice will call in the night darkness which we must follow because we cannot say No.

The next time we say, "You know, the devil made me do that," we need to remember that God is standing by and in effect is shaking his head and saying, "No! No one can make you fall. I will not allow you to be tempted above your ability to resist it."

*Step Three*: God gives avenues of escape. Picture yourself completely surrounded and outnumbered by the enemy. The situation looks hopeless. Then the voice of God comes offering us a proposition. "I will show you a way out of this *if* you are determined to win. But if you are content to surrender, then there is no way to escape."

Temptation begins to encircle us. We can feel ourselves being drawn and enticed. We feel we have reason to hate someone. We start feeling jealous. We begin to plot against a fellow worker. We start to spread a rumor we picked up. Then God comes to the rescue and warns us off. He offers us at least two good avenues of escape.

1. *Stand and fight.* We look temptation squarely in the eye and say, "By the power of God I will not fall to you." Then we can still walk among those who hate without becoming one of them, among those who slander others without our joining in.

In order to be strong enough to stand and fight we have to be convinced of a couple of things. First, that the struggle is worth winning, that we are not willing to be dragged down to natural sordid instincts. Second, that God stands solidly behind us to give us the strength to fight and win.

"Resist the devil and he will flee from you" (James 4:7).

2. *Get up and run.* There are some temptations which we cannot afford to fool with. If we flirt and tease certain temptations, we play too close to the fire. The Bible tells us to do a lot of running. "Flee youthful lusts," "Flee idolatry," "Flee fornication." Each of us needs to know when to fight and when to run, and not to confuse the two.

Yet to be perfectly honest, there are times when this whole temptation thing seems ridiculous. If God is so powerful to protect us, why in the world doesn't he just go *zap!* and remove temptation from the world and get us off the hook?

Doubtless God has thought about this option. If he wanted to he could keep all of us in a padded, isolated cell without temptation. Maybe there would be no one to talk to and nothing to think about.

Yet God had a better plan. People do not grow and mature unless they meet resistance and have to make choices. Consequently God throws some choices into the pot. Then God tells us that through the trials of making choices our faith will be refined and we will grow in Jesus Christ (I Pet. 1:6,7).

# 21

## Sometimes I Feel Like a Hypocrite

It would be difficult to imagine a more obscene word than "hypocrite." Our ears have long ago become accustomed to sordid remarks which insult us, our parents, and our friends. We have heard vulgarities and expletives both privately and publicly, but few words are able to cut into our hearts as bitterly as being labeled a pretender.

No wonder then that in our moments of self-defacing we are likely to turn the word on ourselves. Before we throw this descriptive around too freely we need to lay some ground rules.

Some people very definitely are hypocrites. It is less than helpful to try to assure everyone that they are not. Jesus Christ met some and he quickly identified them as being part of that actors' guild (Matt. 23).

However, we have a right to know that if a person thinks he is a hypocrite he probably is not one. The hypocrite is not the person who self-incriminates. He is not a person given to introspection or self-evaluation. The hypocrite is the person who has decided to "stonewall" it. He may have doubts and inconsistencies but he sees the purpose in life as one of appearances. Do I look righteous, cool, and controlled? Whether or not I really am is not the question.

The key word is *appearance*, not *sincerity*. Many Christians have been harassed by two questions, "What will people say?" and "How would that look?" While these may be valid questions, they often become absurd. A child asks if he can attend a movie and the parents ask, "What will people say?" and not, "Is it good, bad, or neutral?" A pastor once asked his congregation if they would move their Wednesday night program to the basement of the church to give it greater flexibility. It was vetoed on the grounds that the sanctuary lights would be off and the people in the town would think they had gone "liberal." The question was not, Is the program good, helpful or, effective? but, How will it look?

This was certainly the concern of Christ when he addressed the Pharisees in Matthew 23. He accused them of washing the outside of the cup and dish while leaving the inside corrupt and ugly. They were like whitewashed tombs, where inside there was only death (vss. 25–28).

The cry against hypocrisy is really a cry for honesty in a person's relationship with God and man. How many times have we discussed prayer with a group of Christians? They can make exalted statements about the comfort of communicating with God and how prayer changes things. Then what a surprise to poll the group and discover that most of them do not pray regularly. Instead of getting to the heart of the matter and discussing the difficulties of prayer and why people don't pray, we are entangled at the pretense level. We are dealing with the platitudes of our imagination rather than the realities of life.

Possibly we can understand the problem better by seeing it in a different context. The chief priests were looking for a way to trap Christ so they collected some men and sent them as spies to hear the Nazarene. They asked him questions about paying taxes and they "pretended to be honest" (Luke 20:20) when in fact they were something else.

The hypocrite has learned to simulate goodness. When we have our picture taken we often hope the studio will simulate it or touch it up to make us look a little better than we are. All simulation or all pretense is not bad. Sometimes when we have a headache we pretend to be comfortable and work at being polite. Some ideas are ludicrous but we hear the person out nevertheless. However, it is when we transfer this attitude into the spiritual and personal life that the problems intensify. When it departs the realm of being civil and enters the arena of deception then it becomes contemptible.

Material on the subject of hypocrisy is scarce, but the best treatment of the problem is found in *The Person Reborn* by Dr. Paul Tournier (New York: Harper and Row, 1966; pp. 61–67). Dr. Tournier equates hypocrisy with formalism, with keeping up appearances. He points out that many young people are hurt when they see their parents being paraded before the church as pious leaders while at home they are unbearable.

While many groups have gone too far stressing sensitivity training and "let it all hang out," Christians may be suffering from "keep it all bottled up" and put on a good show. The person who doubts the existence of God, the person who hates his parents, the person who is cynical toward life needs a place to discuss these things and develop a Christlike attitude. He cannot gain by pretending that everything is all right. We are often concerned about loneliness, and yet there is little to compare with Christian loneliness. Surrounded by people, cushioned by Beatitudes, and soothed by lofty hymns, still we feel empty and abandoned. The Christian should be permitted to take off his mask, tear up his script, come down from his stage, and say, "I am a person."

In a Christian college where people are used to praying before each class commences, a strange incident occurred. The instructor looked at his list of student names and called on the next student in order to lead in prayer. The student surprised everyone by respectfully declining because he did not feel spiritually attuned. Certainly he must be admired for having a greater concern for his inward condition than for the outward appearance.

In the Sermon on the Mount (Matt. 5–7) Christ expressed great concern for those who are dedicated to formalism. They pray, give, and fast only to be seen of men rather than as a genuine expression before God. It is both stifling and poisonous to arrange our lives before God in a way to please men.

A hypocrite is an insensitive person and yet it is the sensitive person who feels like the hypocrite. The fact is that we are all inconsistent, that most of us accept Christ and reject Christ at the same time. Rather than flog ourselves, we need to realize that a true Christian is one who is committed to Christ and grows in following him.

One day Jesus was talking to some overly confident people. They liked to crow about their righteousness and they felt superior toward others. Christ told them the story of two men praying in the Temple. One stood and said, "God, I thank you that I am not like all other men," and then he started to list his spiritual prowess. The second man, a despised tax collector, merely beat himself on the chest and said, "God, have mercy on me, a sinner." Then Jesus drew the moral to the story, "For everyone who exalts himself will be humbled, and he who humbles himself will be exalted" (Luke 18:14).

It would be difficult to find a clearer distinction between hypocrisy and sincerity than Christ's illustration. Yet many of us are too intense in our race to appear pious to search after honesty. Dr. Tournier says that this is particularly true of spiritual leaders who are unwilling to admit that they have spiritual problems because they are afraid they will cause other Christians to fall. They carry a burden greater than God intended for them, because God did not ask them to hold up the scenery to try and make their life look bright.

We can all conclude that we are not hypocrites because we have difficulties. We are merely Christians grappling with our problems and growing in our joy. Knowing that, we are far better off admitting that we are disciples of clay in need of the grace of God than pretending that we have reached a spiritual "utopia."

# 22

## Sometimes I Can't Say No!

Recently a magazine ran an article about a woman who had left her husband. It was a warm, human, but tragic story. He had not been involved in some sordid affair or become part of sensational scandal. He merely got involved in so many good works that he was never home and finally she could no longer take it. She had married a man who couldn't say No to worthy causes.

Nelson Bell wrote in *Christianity Today:* "Many of the troubles and sorrows in the world today are due to someone's inability to say 'No.' " It would be impossible to calculate how much damage has been done by well-meaning people who had never mastered the sanctified "uh-uh."

To many the Christian life has become literally a pressure cooker: the Men's Fellowship pushing from this side and the choir from that; the district relief commission from the north and the Vacation Bible School from the south. What promised to be a life of freedom and service can become a list of demands and hopeless entanglements.

I once saw a book with the intriguing title *Blessed Be the Ties That Free.* Maybe the ties that bind have bound us too tightly, even to the place where the goal of the Christian is to conform to a mold. Naturally life is one of responsibility, of sharing and contributing to others; however, when it is overdone, life becomes a stifling mess.

Romans 12:2 teaches us to "not conform any longer to the pattern of this world, but be transformed by the renewing of your mind." Would it be unfair to apply this verse to the religious world? If we simply conform to what every other Christian wants us to do, where is the freedom to follow Christ? Possibly some of us are very unimaginative and unadventurous in our walk with God because we look around and conform to what we already see. The Wright brothers could not fly by breeding horses. They had to learn to say No to existing demands in order to rise above them.

Christ's pattern of life shows a steady ability to draw the line. People came to him and said, "Why don't your disciples fast like other disciples?" In effect, Christ replied No; he would not conform to someone else's way of life (Mark 2:18). After the resurrection his own disciples felt frustrated because they wanted him to establish his kingdom. He refused to be pressured into complying to the whims and wishes of others (Acts 1:7).

I met a lady in the hospital who had not attended church for a few years. She spoke of her genuine conversion experience and how she started to attend a local church. The people were so friendly that quickly she was bombarded with invitations to attend this and to serve on that. Soon the kind and open attitude turned into a persistence and grew in intensity. People began to worry about her because she was missing at this function or that event. Instead of a fellowship it became a hassle and she eventually felt that the only relief was to bail out.

How many tired and weary casualties there are who were wounded in the Christian blitz: pounded from the pulpit, pelted from the pew, kicked in the kitchen, clobbered by the club, corralled by the choir, fleeced by the fellowship, and battered by the board. Well-meaning people and many worthy causes, but deadly to the person who lacks the self-control to say No.

God intended that we enjoy the good things of life and not merely be overwhelmed with responsibility. "So I conclude that, first, there is nothing better for a man than to be happy and to enjoy himself as long as he can; and second, that he should eat and drink and enjoy the fruits of his labors, for these are gifts from God" (Eccles. 3:12–13).

Part of the dilemma faced by many is the constant clamor to get more done. Christian groups are compared with retail stores and a certain amount of work must be efficiently done. Growth, activity, production. Maybe the whole emphasis is misplaced. Someone has suggested that if a person teaches a Sunday school class, possibly that is all he should do in Christian service. To do that task well is better than doing a dozen jobs poorly.

Groups tend to take themselves too seriously. The school system feels it must do everything for the student. The baseball leagues think that the dedicated child will push aside life and limb to practice constantly. The church joins the chorus and fills up nights with services, committee meetings, and social functions. People on the run. The effect on the person who cannot say No is disastrous. Where is the time to pursue other adventures? Where is the time to think and create? And if we are not careful the net effect of the church will be to withdraw all Christians from community activities in order to cluster them under the shadow of the sanctuary.

The Bible gives an excellent formula for a person to measure his own strides and know how far he can go. "Each man should test his own actions. Then he can take pride in himself, without comparing himself to somebody else, for each man should carry his own load" (Gal. 6:4,5).

If we allow other people to tell us what we can do and what we must do, we are likely to become bent out of shape. Every man must learn to carry his own cargo and do what he knows is his lot. If he tries to match other people and keep their pace, he is destined for unhappiness, even agony.

Some years ago I was invited to speak at a banquet. The people hoped to inaugurate a Men's Fellowship in the church and wanted a vivacious challenge to stir the hearts of men and spur them on to enormous heights.

Much to the chairman's embarrassment I outlined six reasons why you should not have a Men's Fellowship. If they could answer these objections and deficits, then by all means full speed ahead.

In many places such a group can be an excellent help, but only too often it becomes a vice, a vice which slowly twists tighter and firmer until it is impossible for one to escape. What may begin as a progressive and even innovative concept soon degenerates into an unimaginative institution. What is initiated as a free, spirited form of ministry has a tendency to gravitate into a press group. "Let's get out and support it." "Aren't you coming Saturday night?" "If we don't get behind this it isn't going to work." How many Christians want to scream out against such often unnecessary, family-crushing, personality-shattering, freedom-robbing organization?

Basic to the freedom which every Christian deserves is changing our responsibilities into opportunities. Attending church is not that awesome obligation which everyone must do or risk serious divine incrimination. Church services in multicolored variety are opportunities to grow, to serve, even to repose. They become a burden when they are offered under the gun.

Does the church exist for the people or do the people exist for the church? Some churches merely create jobs and organizations and then demand that the people support them. Every Christian should have the healthy options of a positive No. Maybe even a No, thank you, but a No nevertheless.

Sometimes we are driven to overextend ourselves because of our guilt feelings. We do not feel good about ourselves unless we drive ourselves beyond our limits. We can have a much happier life if we measure our noble causes, measure our own abilities and interests, and learn to exercise a very wholesome, sanctified "uh-uh."

# 23

## I Always Need God-Control

There was a young lady who faithfully attended most of the services in her church. Since she had a beautiful voice she was often asked to minister by singing. Her excellent talent caused a lot of problems.

When she sang, people all over the congregation would look at the floor or just sit there and stare. Her personality had made so many enemies that many people simply could not stand to hear her sing.

Seeing this her pastor invited her to come and talk about the situation. Calmly the minister outlined the problem as he saw it and asked what she thought could be done about it.

Her reply was crisp, "Pastor, I read my Bible every morning and between you and me I think I'm all right."

Someone had taught her that the Christian life consisted of reading the Bible. But somehow she failed to learn that it takes a close walk with God to bring about a factual change in our attitudes, our actions, and our treatment of other people.

It is possible to hear fifty to two hundred sermons a year and see no actual change in our contentment or our behavior. This is true because neither knowledge nor activity can give to us what we receive by having the Holy Spirit of God control our lives.

Every Christian who has lost his enthusiasm, his zip, and his consistency could benefit from reading the simplicity of Ephesians 5:18: "Do not get drunk on wine which leads to debauchery. Instead be filled with the Spirit."

We must identify what kind of experience we are talking about. Being controlled by the Spirit is not a "super" Christian experience reserved for monks in Spain. Nor is it necessarily an emotional experience that will lead one to do cartwheels in the parking lot. Being filled or controlled by the Holy Spirit is something that the everyday struggling Christian can have.

Many Christians have tried very hard to find peace in the Christian life by *doing* everything correctly. Attend this, hear him, read that, serve on the committee. All of it may be excellent but it helps very little if a basic principle is ignored. It is more important to be than to do.

How often have we been turned off by a "busy" Christian? He does everything, he thinks he knows everything, and he is steamrolling in every direction. Yet somehow we get the feeling that he has bypassed the peace of God and traded it for activity. He could be helped a lot by Psalm 46:10: "Stand silent! Know that I am God!" (LIVING BIBLE). It is more important to be than to do.

When an individual becomes a Christian the Holy Spirit comes inside and lives there. The Holy Spirit is not a special gift but a normal resident of the believer. Romans 8:9 says: "And if anyone does not have the Spirit of Christ, he does not belong to Christ."

Since we became Christians the Holy Spirit has been doing a great many things for us. He is busy encouraging us when we get blue or things are tough. He teaches us from the Bible and sometimes he convicts when we are wrong. He gives us vim, vigor and, often, stability.

As all Christians do, it is not long before we start fouling things up. We make mistakes, we say the wrong thing, we sin. At this point the Holy Spirit backs off. He still lives in us but he is grieved by what we have done (Eph. 4:30). He is much like the rest of us in that he has been working hard trying to help us and we have thrown cold water on his efforts (I Thess. 5:19). Often we can feel it. Something is not right between ourselves and God. There is a chill in our spiritual life.

The first step to actual Spirit-control is to identify our problem, our cause for estrangement, and then do something about it. It may mean apologizing to a friend we hurt, giving up a practice of ours, or confessing something to God. But wherever we know there is a chill between us and God, it needs to be taken care of. Often it is the refusal of the Christian to take this step of cleansing which robs him of the happy Christian life.

If we drive a nail into our hand, the wound will not heal properly unless it is first cleaned out. The Spirit-controlled life works on the same principle.

However, the key to the filling of the Spirit is not merely negative. It does not come only because we have removed the hindrances. The filling or control of the Spirit is a positive action. A conscious choice. It is an attitude, an invitation, a yielding, and maybe even an asking. We want the Spirit to take over our life.

Many people become discouraged because they are afraid that Spirit-control really means perfection, and most of us know we are not perfect. But be encouraged. It may well be possible to be partially filled: 50 percent, 65 percent, 90 percent.

Suppose a person has eliminated many forms of hate and envy and lying, and yet he still has one problem. He cannot stand left-handed Lithuanians. They make his blood boil.

While this is a problem and needs to be corrected, is it not possible that the Spirit fills the rest of his life? This gives all of us hope for at least a large degree of Spirit-control. Naturally we do not aim for partial control, but we realize that 65 percent is progress and we reach for 75 percent. What can a person expect to receive from Spirit-control? One Christian said, "Before I understood Spirit-control I could not recommend the Christian life. I wasn't sure I wanted someone else to join my misery." The control of the Spirit dramatically changed his life.

The person who invites the Spirit to rule over every part of his life can expect concrete change. He can expect his attitude and outlook to improve. In short he can expect to feel better. Some Christians are afraid of the word "feeling," but they need not be.

Consider what Paul told us in verses 19, 20, and 21 of Ephesians 5. After the control he tells us to have a melody in our heart to the Lord. He tells us to be thankful to God and to submit ourselves to each other. What happened to grouchiness, petty arguments, and bitterness? We feel better about ourselves, about our friends, and about God.

Would we like to be at peace, to have joy, to feel love, to have patience? These are genuine, personal, practical feelings and Galatians 5:22 says they belong to us as the fruit of the Spirit. These words have been in our vocabulary for a long time, but often they are empty and meaningless. The words are useless unless a feeling goes with them.

Someone says he has joy. Yet is he grumpy, quick-tempered, and outwardly miserable.

"How do you know you have joy?"

"The Bible says I have joy."

"Where do you have joy?"

"Deep down in my soul."

Can a soul be so deep that you can have joy without feeling it? Or are some people playing a game of words in order to cover up a sad soul?

A conscious invitation to have the Holy Spirit of God control our life can bring about a dramatic change which can make life the full, exciting experience the Bible promises it to be.

# 24

===

# *Will Everything Really Work Out?*

A young doctor drowned just months before he was scheduled to leave for the mission field. The Christians who heard about this were shocked almost to disbelief that such potential could be wasted in an accident. For many Christians their minds moved naturally to the Bible, and Romans 8:28 soon came to mind. After all, everything does work together for good to those who love God. Yet, sometimes it is a hard passage to understand and accept.

The verse sounds good. It has a melody about it that reminds one of a poem and it has almost a cleansing quality. Even if we do not comprehend it, we all like to think it is true. It is a secret wish that in the end everything turns out fine.

But what does the famous passage, Romans 8:28, really mean? A man who lost his wife in an accident said, "A lot of people have quoted this verse to me, but I don't think they really know what it says."

Maybe a look at it through a microscope will help all of us to appreciate the true worth of the promise.

Let us begin by recognizing what it does *not* say. The Bible does not teach that God causes everything to happen. If we need proof of this, sometime put your hand on a table and stab it with a knife. As the blood gushes up and you search for a Band-aid tell yourself two theological truths:

One, God did not stab you in the hand.

Two, God did not stop you from stabbing yourself in the hand.

God gets blamed for a lot of things in life for which he is not responsible. It is a cop-out to blame God for all the blunders and tragedies that happen to men. Romans 8:28 does not say this and we should not assume it.

A second thing which the verse is accused of but does not say is that all things are good. All things are *not* good. Both the Word of God and our conscience tells us this.

Millions of Africans are starving. Can we say to ourselves, "It is good that Africans are starving to death?" Such logic violates our moral senses.

If a mother of six children suffers a mental breakdown and spends a year in an institution, should we call it good? It would be good if she could have stayed home and loved her family.

Isaiah 5:20: "Woe unto them who call evil, good."

There is no doubt that God causes some tragedies in life but he does not cause all of them. Suppose a man has an infected foot and refuses to care for it. If finally the foot is amputated, do we then say, "I wonder what reason God has for taking his foot?" There may be no lofty cause or spiritual platitude but, rather, the negligence of man.

The power of Romans 8:28 is that God can take all things, even man's clumsy blunders, and turn them into good. Use of this fact will allow us to turn life's defeats into victories.

Paul claims that "we know"—dogmatic statement made with great certainty. How do Paul and others know that all things work together for good? By personal experience they watched God turn things around. Also by revelation we are all assured of the promises in the verse.

The apostle continues to speak in absolutes by including the broadest possible scope—"all things." Death and injury to be sure, but also the tiny specks of life like a torn coat or a lost five-dollar bill.

A young man once stole $80 and was caught. All of life seemed to stand still for a sad moment in a gifted person's life. Yet from that horror he rose again to marry a wonderful woman and to carry on an active ministry among young people.

"All things" is limited only by our imagination and willingness to give it a try in the hands of God.

This verse does not include a magic wand or promise us an angel sitting at the foot of our hospital bed. Rather, God tells us that things will work for good. Work implies energy and effort being spent by someone. If we decide to sit and sulk about our problem, maybe God will just let us. God is willing to work, but the Christian who sits and does nothing may sit for a long time.

The person who is turned down by medical school has some decisions to make. If God is to work this rejection into something good, the student has to get off the park bench, lift up his head, and be willing to move. God does send some chariots to pick up people, but amazingly few.

The power of God is the basic strength to this work, but the verse does not imply roosting Christians.

A young seminary student's wife had a miscarriage, and the disappointment and gloom were heavy. Yet the husband could see through the darkness and say, "Someday I'll be able to minister to others because of what we've been through."

This miscarriage was terrible, but he was determined to work it out for good.

We have a definite handicap in not being able to see the total picture of life. God says things work together. Puzzles are made up of pieces, but one piece is often little understood.

How many can remember having a serious crush on someone at seventeen? Then she gave you back the ring, told you to go hang—and the world seemed to end. At that moment it was a serious blow and a great heartache. Yet today looking back at one's total life, it really meant little in the complete picture. It is difficult to evaluate the good derived from an incident until we see the larger perspective.

Paul and Silas went to jail, and incarceration could have been terrible. God worked it together for good, and the jailer was happy they had come that way.

God has a concept of good which often differs from ours. Prosperity, success, vitality all seem to fit our goals in life, but God may have a different standard. The Christian with a passion for Christ will learn to look for Christ's definition of good and find great satisfaction in it.

Very possibly we will not know how God worked something out for good until we are with him. And if he does not care to tell us, then that will be perfectly fine also.

While God can be called the father of all mankind, the promises here are not given to everyone. Only certain people fit under this umbrella and God tells us who they are: those who love him and are called according to his purpose.

Those who cannot trust him and are disinterested in his purpose are obviously left in the rain.

Imagine going to a body-and-fender shop to have a car fixed. After you ask the man if he can repair the car, the proprietor puts his arm around you and says, "Friend, you have had no accident. There are no accidents in life. Your car has only been rearranged." You look at your crushed grill, twisted bumper, shattered windshield, and wonder if the man is dangerous.

God does not tell us that we have had no injuries, heartbreaks, or tragedies in life. Everything is not good. But if we love him enough to trust him, he will change that wreck of life into something good and worthwhile  God, we are ready. Where do we go from here?